Healing the Planet and Ourselves

How to Raise Your Vibration

Michele Doucette

Healing the Planet and Ourselves: How to Raise Your Vibration

Copyright © 2011 by Michele Doucette, St. Clair Publications

All rights reserved. No part of this publication may be reproduced or transmitted in any form or by any means, electronic or mechanical, including photocopying, recording, or by any information storage and retrieval system, without written permission from the author.

ISBN 978-1-935786-07-8

Printed in the United States of America by

St. Clair Publications

PO Box 726

McMinnville, TN   37111-0726

http://stan.stclair.net

Dedicated to Claudette (Ravenmoonstar) Kennedy, a fellow soul sister, who passed away on October 29, 2010. Privy to many online metaphysical conversations, it was an honor to have reconnected with her in this lifetime. I shall always be grateful for the strength of the relationship that we forged in such a short time. Truly this is also an important and essential part of what we have come here to experience.

As spoken by the Dalai Lama, *the highest happiness is when one reaches the stage of liberation, at which there is no more suffering.* May you now enjoy this time of much earned liberation, my dearest, dearest friend.

Acknowledgments

I wish to thank Shaun George for permission to use his *Perseverance* photograph in that it just seemed to be the most apt visual for the cover of this book. Likewise, the word itself also sums everything up rather nicely.

http://www.flickr.com/photos/23641763@N08

In terms of healing myself, I continue to persevere. In terms of healing the planet, this can only happen as each individual heals themselves. All comes to fruition in the proper aligning of one's vibrational energies.

As the reader delves into this book, they will quickly come to the realization that this is not your typical metaphysical volume.

While it is one that focuses on the alignment of vibrational energies, that lead to healing, as many others do, it is also one that has involved considerable assistance from the mineral kingdom, for it is their words that have been put to paper.

In this light, I wish to thank my countless crystal companions. Given their deep connection to Mother Earth, their input (via meditation) was most appreciated.

I trust that the reader shall enjoy this unique departure from the course of my previous works. Truly, I am in awe of this particular manifestation.

Table of Contents

Reviews 1

Introduction 9

Siberian Charoite 13

Selenite 16

Turquoise 19

Lapis Lazuli 23

Red Jasper 26

Green Tiger Chalcedony 31

Pink Petalite 33

Libyan Desert Glass 35

Iolite 39

Larimar 41

Dominican Amber 44

Bronzite 48

Septarian 51

Calavera Stone 54

Star Rose Quartz 57

Green Grossular Garnet 62

Smoky Quartz with Black Tourmaline 65

Lemurian Seed Crystals	69
Spider Jasper	73
Labradorite	76
Ametrine	80
Golden C	84
Rainbow Mayanite Quartz	88
Ajoite	90
Dragon's Blood Granite	92
Petrified Peanut Wood	96
Sonora Sunrise	99
Nuummite	102
Anorthosite	106
Covellite	108
Russian Quartz Record Keeper	112
Blue Celestite	117
Quantum Quattro Silica	120
Citrine	125
Serpentine	129
Black Obsidian	134
Shattuckite	138
Apophyllite Pyramid	141
Dioptase	143

Black Tourmaline 145

Atlantisite 149

Verdite 154

Purple Jade 158

Kunzite 161

Hiddenite 164

Malachite 167

Hematite 170

Red Petrified Wood 173

Sunstone 177

Seraphinite 185

Jet 189

Lithium Quartz 192

Copper 196

Carnelian 199

Copper Royale 203

Rutilated Quartz 207

Chrysocolla 209

Lepidolite with Pink Rubellite 215

Wild Horse Picture Jasper 219

Ruby with Kyanite 222

Youngite 225

Amethyst DT Brandberg Channeling Crystal 229

Healer's Gold 232

Tibetan DT Quartz 234

Satyaloka Quartz 238

Red Celestial Candle Quartz 240

Faden Quartz 243

Red Rosetta Stone 247

Dragon's Blood Jasper 251

Rainforest Jasper 254

Clear Quartz Cathedral 257

Amazonite 261

Blue Lace Agate 263

Rainbow Fluorite 265

Aqua Aura Spirit Quartz 269

Moldavite 273

Herkimer Diamond 276

Clear Quartz 278

Eudialyte 282

Scepter Quartz Crystal 286

Prehnite 288

Variscite 291

Rhodonite 294

Lazulite 296

Sugilite 299

Moonstone 301

Phenacite 303

Chiastolite 307

Super Seven 309

Nebula Stone 311

Chrysoprase 313

Tangerine Quartz 315

Moss Agate 316

Amethyst 318

Selenite Rose 322

Angelite 324

Blue Apatite 326

Aquamarine 328

Azurite 331

Mangano Calcite 333

Fulgurite 335

Garnet 337

Pyrite 340

Unakite 342

Green Tourmaline 345

Pink Tourmaline	348
Watermelon Tourmaline	351
Fossilized Dinosaur Bone	353
Azeztulite	358
Citrine Azeztulite	361
Left and Right Activation Crystal	363
Lithium Based Stones	366
Nano Wand	368
The Continuum of Sound®	371
Astrology Related	375
Metaphysical Property Sites	379
Concluding Message	381
Bibliography	389
About the Author	398

Reviews

In this unique tome, *Healing the Planet and Ourselves: How to Raise Your Vibration*, spiritual author, Michele Doucette, extols in vivid detail, from personal experience as well as extensive research, the virtues, energies and healing qualities of an enormous number of crystals, gemstones, metals and petrified woods, all in relation to their affect on the human experience.

Many of these minerals have been in use for thousands of years; others were discovered as late as the 19th and 20th centuries.

Herein, Michele also invites the reader's mind to examine the legends and mysteries handed down to us by our forebears.

In addition, many truths come into play concerning the varieties of each stone that the average person has likely never heard of.

Healing the Planet and Ourselves

I personally found it interesting to denote that Hematite (iron oxide), often used in jewelry and widely known for its healing powers, has also been found on the planet Mars. I was also intrigued to discover that Lepidolite is a by-product of mining lithium, which certainly has a multitude of uses in today's world of technology.

Each chapter is concluded with a key word or thought.

As I combed through the fascinating pages of this book, I found myself entranced; so much so, in fact, that I soon began taking notes. Thinking about stories that had been relayed to me in the past, I began wondering if, and how, they might possibly be connected to Michele's findings.

Certain words and thoughts stand out with ringing truth.

One such case is found in her chapter on Lapis Lazuli, a stone that was highly revered in ancient Egypt, so greatly, in fact, as to overlay the sarcophagus of King Tut. Here, great importance is given to the balancing of both masculine and feminine energies.

Another is found in her chapter on Star Rose Quartz, where love is shown to be the all-important virtue which guides us through life — "love is the answer."

Another stand-out is in the Golden C chapter — "positivity is key."

In the chapter on Sonora Sunrise, found in Mexico — "all is energy" strikes a chord.

There are simply too many thought-provoking truisms to mention even a fraction of them here. Likewise, her probing questions are piercing.

For the novice, this book can be the gateway to the study of harmony in the human spirit, addressing how spiritual attributes such as wisdom, individual truth, positive energy, peace, love, forgiveness and spiritual destiny can be obtained, in part, through meditation as an experiential method; a method that can be utilized singularly (on its own) and/or enhanced with various minerals (as discussed within).

Healing the Planet and Ourselves

For the more aware individual, someone who is looking for a greater explanation of these fascinating stones and minerals, Michele offers a deep and thorough study, whilst still keeping the terminology on a level that can be understood, and appreciated, by all.

To get the full thrust of this book, as in the old adage, *you just had to be there*, this is a volume that you simply have to read for yourself. In so doing, you will have embarked on an inspiring, passionate and illuminating journey into understanding and mastering the inner self. In short, you will learn to "become what you have always been," so that you may learn to concentrate on the things that really matter in life.

Stanley J. St. Clair, author of *Prayers of Prophets, Knights and Kings* and *Mysterious People of the Bible in the Light of History*

Healing the Planet and Ourselves

It is hard for me to put into words what your writing means to me because it is so good, to the point, and yet full of hope for the future.

I feel that you recognize the need to raise our vibration for positive endeavors and through doing the work, one can actually change the way they process information to change their lives for the better ... this gives me goosebumps in the most positive of ways!

You are such a commendable writer, Michele. I find it truly amazing that you manage to write so many books at once; you must live in a creative vortex. I can see that many will flock to your latest work on crystals.

Kellie Jo Conn, The Crystal Deva
http://www.neatstuff.net/avalon/

Healing the Planet and Ourselves

Once again, this time through meditation, intuition and the guidance of a significant number of crystals and stones, Michele has captured another exceptional volume. Until the time comes when all can listen like Michele has done, we can read and feel the words of wisdom as shared herein, courtesy of these mineral beings.

Jean-Guy Poirier, Canada

Such an important book of our time, not only to remind us, and indeed inform those who may not have been aware of our connection, a very ancient connection, and even a re-connection for some ... to these ancient beings, these crystals and minerals ... a reminder that we were connected in the past and indeed need to re-connect at this present time.

They have held all this information for us, until now. It is indeed time to listen and heal ourselves and Mother Earth, for the very Highest Good of all.

Healing the Planet and Ourselves

Along with getting to know these wonderful crystals on many levels, Michele helps us to identify the healing that is needed. As I was engaged in learning about these magnificent, energy filled, beings of the mineral world, I also felt as if I was receiving my very own personal spiritual reading to go (as an added bonus).

What a wonderful concept for a book. This is something I have never seen before, in one work. There are, indeed, many books out there with information on crystals, their properties and qualities, but this is quite different; this one is unique.

Between Michele's meditations with each crystal, and their sharing of many messages, filled with inspiration, and guidance, for humanity, this is a truly brilliant work.

I, too, am a guardian of crystals. Always looking for additional information, as a way of getting to know them better, I feel that there is much to be discovered here, in this wonderful new reference book, especially in keeping with their shared words.

Healing the Planet and Ourselves

Throughout the reading of this book, I was surprised to come across information, much of which was new to me, but I was equally as intrigued to discover crystals that I had not before been familiar with.

As I was reading the different chapters, I found myself reaching for those particular crystals. I felt the energy re-awakening on a supplementary level, much akin to when you learn something new about an old friend, thereafter looking upon them with enhanced admiration.

While this book is so vastly different from Michele's other works, I found it to be just as inspiring. Each time I finish another, I am pleased to be able to share that she has been successful in helping me see life in a whole new light.

This is a book that I would encourage all to read, whether or not they have a connection, or an affinity, with crystals.

It was a blessing to read this book and I know that you, the reader, will also be able to find the same, and more, with each successive reading.

Suzi Cullen, Australia

Introduction

As Anastasia of the Siberian tiaga has stated throughout the Ringing Cedars series, *Man is Creator*. In keeping, so, too, is God Creator.

It is my personal belief that God(dess) is thought; henceforth, thought is also Creator. After all, was not the beginning stated as being the word? What was word, then, if not thought?

Man, therefore, creates his (her) own reality through thought. It all comes down to *what does Man wish to create*, does it not?

Thought is tangible. All of my previous publications, resulting from thought, can be physically held by you, the reader, for they are *materialized* thought.

Crystals represent the heart, the inner soul, of the Great Mother. With regards to this publication, I sat with eyes closed in meditation, in an attempt to connect with the energies of the crystals.

Healing the Planet and Ourselves

When holding an individual crystal in my left hand, I am able to feel their energetic vibration. At the same time, my right hand often vibrates deeply, almost as if the energy of the crystal is demanding to be released in words. Doing my utmost as a spiritual translator, I put forth a request to the stones, asking them to tell me what it was that I needed to know.

We live in a world "with a chaotic energy field, created by electronics around us. Modern conveniences such as cell phones, computers and microwaves, emit radiation and electromagnetic waves that interfere with our bodies' magnetic fields. Fortunately, nature has given us the gift of gemstones, whose organic energies help us return to our natural healthy state." [1]

In order to gain the full benefits attributed to gemstones, meaning energies that can extend outward from the physical body up to approximately one foot in diameter, they need to be worn.

---

[1] Carnelian Gemstone Meaning, Healing Properties and History website accessed on January 13, 2011 at http://wishgiving.com/gems/carnelian-gemstone-meaning.html

Healing the Planet and Ourselves

Gemstone jewelry, then, is the most convenient way to maintain the electromagnetic field surrounding the body, without the need for invasive medical procedures.

When I want a special wire wrapped stone, I call upon the amazing talent of Crystalmoon (Barbara Allen) of Crystal Moon Jewelry Designs. [2]

When I want a beaded necklace (with many choices of stone type, stone size and style), interfaced with hand tied knots and silver toggle clasps, I call upon Mandy's Gemstones. [3]

Aside from carrying specific stones in my pocket (all of which are housed in a cotton bag), these are the gemstone jewelry sellers on eBay that I purchase from on a regular basis.

Knowing that the vibratory power of stones has been held in high esteem by many throughout the ages, it should come as no surprise that they have been studied extensively.

---

[2] http://stores.ebay.ca/Crystal-Moon-Jewelry-Designs
[3] http://stores.ebay.ca/Mandys-Gemstones

Healing the Planet and Ourselves

While this book is one of metaphysical study, it is *not* a resource whereby you will discover the specific properties and powers associated with the stones types addressed herein; instead, it is a meditative and reflective study, all of which has been based on personal experience(s).

As my husband is so fond of saying ... *One needs to live many lives in order to discern the value of now.* I trust that this resource shall assist you with your own individual discernment.

Siberian Charoite

It has been said that Charoite is a deeply spiritual stone. Purple in color, it can be attributed to the activation of the Crown chakra (the chakra that enables us to communicate with our spiritual nature, as in one's Higher Self, God Self, God Source).

I find Charoite to be an extremely powerful stone; a stone of purity that interfaces with the pure of heart (thought as well as intention). I feel much serenity when meditating with this stone.

Many of you do not like who you are, let alone love who you are. It is of the utmost importance that you learn to love yourself, that you learn to accept all facets of yourself, for together they create the totality of you.

You are much too hard on yourselves. In truth, you are beings of divine sovereignty. We understand the choices that you have made, to experience anew without the remembering.

Healing the Planet and Ourselves

We commend you for your efforts in wanting to expand your knowledge, to expand your understanding, for all is continually evolving, but now is also the time for you to embrace, with complete acceptance, the totality of you.

You must seek out that special place, a place where you can go to appreciate and experience the stillness. You must free yourselves from the linear driven schedules that control from sunrise to sundown.

You must seek out this special place every day. This must become your time; a time away from TVs, computers, cell phones, laptops, blackberries.

Freedom and peace of mind are to be found within the stillness, if you but allow yourself to venture forth. The final choice, however, always rests with you.

We can only offer reflective words.

As a being from the mineral kingdom, we rejoice when the human makes an effort to connect with us because each is here to experience harmony in accordance with the other.

Healing the Planet and Ourselves

In keeping with your crystalline journey, we are here to assist you. Know that you are loved by the totality of all creation.

Know that you are not alone, that you have never been alone. We have been here waiting for your very return; the return to your divine selves.

aka Serenity

Selenite

Selenite is a white stone connected to the balancing of the Crown chakra (the chakra that enables us to communicate with our spiritual nature, as in one's Higher Self, God Self, God Source). It has also been shared that Selenite is a stone that opens and activates the Soul Star chakra (located immediately above the Crown chakra and dubbed the *seat of the soul* chakra).

Illumination pertains to clear understanding, awareness, enlightenment, truth. When one lives their truth, one knows peace of mind. The question that bodes asking ... *what is truth* ... is the same for everyone. Meditating with this stone always seems to draw me closer to that which is my truth.

We love it when you begin to think outside the box, asking of yourself what is truth, for you have embarked on the road to divinity. There exists only one truth that encompasses all, and that truth is love.

Healing the Planet and Ourselves

What is it that brings one to their individual truth(s)? Experience is of extreme importance, for all serve to enhance one's vision of truth. This is a process that has spanned millennia and will continue to do so.

A great many of you call yourselves ancients, and so it is. Likewise, we, too, are ancients, even including those who have been newly discovered as it were.

In retrospect, we have been waiting for the most opportune time in which to be born, if indeed that is the proper term to be using.

All must become a seeker of their own truth. Cease delegating your power to any so-called authority outside of yourself. Seek that which resides within, for therein you shall discover your truth.

It is important to denote that what you define as truth may be vastly different from the truth of another. So, too, is this truth. Compassion and nonjudgment become integral components of one's inherent truth(s).

Healing the Planet and Ourselves

Having been born of the same consciousness, it should become apparent to you that we are all the same consciousness; a consciousness birthed in love, allowing each to experience itself subjectively.

It is this consciousness of love (some call it God) that allows each to further the expansion of creation. Is this not a tremendous gift that all have been given?

This is why experiences are unique to the individual. One cannot judge what one does not understand and has never experienced. The choices made by another belong to that being of light, to be experienced in totality.

Embrace the oneness while taking the time to celebrate the diversity that life offers. To love life is to love the totality of all creation. It is important, herein, to come back to love. In truth, love is all there is.

aka Illuminator

Turquoise

A stone most revered by Indigenous peoples, Turquoise can be used to activate the Throat chakra (linked to our ability to communicate). Beads dating back to 5000 BC were located in Iraq. The Egyptians were mining Turquoise in the Sinai desert in 3200 BC. As you can see, there exists quite the history with respect to this stone.

I always feel an inherent connection with both Mother Earth and Father Sky when spending time with this stone.

Mother Earth and Father Sky; these words make us smile, for we also resonate with them. To become one with these creators, means becoming one with nature. Living in harmony with nature is so very important, especially in these difficult and challenging times.

Take the time to experience the sunrise, heralding the beginning of each new day. Feel the warmth of the rays of the sun as it caresses your skin with its fingertips.

Healing the Planet and Ourselves

Likewise, take the time to watch the sunset, a time of rest and rejuvenation for all, nature included. Feel the coolness of the moon as it lights a path for all to see.

Spend time with the trees, for they are your brothers and sisters. These long standing ancient ones have many stories to share, meant for those who will but take the time to listen.

When you need grounding, come to the trees. Ask them for their assistance. Sit with them. Spend time in solitude with them. Thank them for their shelter. Thank them for their shade. Do not be afraid to hug them if you feel beckoned to do so. You need the trees as much as they need you.

Walking barefoot across the grass is another way in which to reconnect with Mother Earth. See your roots extending deep into her physical body where all is safe. As well, see your roots extending from Mother Earth up into the heavens, coming back to you, full circle. With a circle, there is no beginning and no end; there is merely infinity. Embrace this infinity without fear.

Healing the Planet and Ourselves

Take the time to smell the flowers. Immerse yourself in their fragrant beauty. Surround yourself with their wondrous color, working the soil with your hands.

Take the time to appreciate the breezes that cool and the rains that nourish.

Take the time to acknowledge the warmth of the sun as it enhances the life of all living beings. Likewise for the moon, as its gravitational attraction controls the tides, most important for the navigation of your oceans.

Take the time to be cognizant of the waters of the earth, remembering that water responds to the power of words.

It is through the work of Dr. Masaru Emoto that water has been shown to have the ability to absorb, hold and retain human feelings and emotions.

Remembering that the human body is comprised of a significant percentage of water, therein lies the alchemical connection of water to individual and collective consciousness.

Healing the Planet and Ourselves

Knowing that certain words can enhance one's immunity, is this not representative of the fact that one can heal themselves through the power of words?

Nature is to be enjoyed, to be honored.

Reconnecting with nature is akin to reconnecting with that part of yourself that has long been lost.

We are here to welcome you back.

aka Sonora

Lapis Lazuli

Lapis Lazuli is a stone that has been attributed to ancient Egypt, found in scarabs, beads, pendants and other jewelry as far back as 3100 BC. Research has also uncovered that the sarcophagus of Pharaoh Tutankhamen was richly inlaid with Lapis Lazuli. Many burial ornaments of Egyptian pharaohs and queens were also carved from this stone. It is very easy to see how this particular stone quickly became synonymous with royalty.

Associated with the Brow (Third Eye) chakra (the avenue to intuitive wisdom, also referenced as second sight), it is this stone that has been ascribed to the developing and/or enhancing of one's intuitive (psychic) powers.

You have been indecisive for far too long. Giving your power away has resulted in complete and total in-action, whereby you have allowed others to think and respond for you. This has allowed you to simply go about your comfortable lives.

Healing the Planet and Ourselves

Day in, day out, never one to challenge the status quo; always willing to accept without dispute, without question. The time for you to emerge as the glorious consciousness that you are, and have always been, is now.

You must learn to delve deeply into that which is you, your consciousness, for therein you shall find that which you have been seeking: none other than your very selves.

You must learn to trust your intuitive self, a most important aspect that has been lost for countless ages.

Some energies are masculine (strong, overpowering) whilst others are feminine (soft, soothing) in nature. As humans, you must learn to balance both of these energies so as not to become too aggressive or too faint hearted.

There must be a blending of the two.

Both are essential, as has long been reflected in the Chinese yin yang symbol.

Balance is an incredibly important word. Where there is balance, there is harmony.

Healing the Planet and Ourselves

Where there is harmony, there is inner peace.

Where there is inner peace, there is compassion.

Where there is compassion, there is freedom of the mind.

All must get back to obtaining this freedom of the mind. Freedom of the mind allows one to think for themselves. It also means that one must take responsibility for that which they create.

When such freedom exists, there is no need for judgment or retribution.

As you obtain this freedom of which you seek, by your example, so shall others be led to explore the same path. You, then, become the light as carried by the hermit, also known as the seeker. Your enlightenment is what shall serve to blaze the path of all who come thereafter.

By their fruits (ways, thoughts, attitudes, actions), ye shall know them.

aka Ma'at

Red Jasper

An amulet of Nefer (a term used to describe goodness and beauty, linked with the Goddess Isis), carved from Red Jasper, is currently housed at the British Museum, dating back to about 1250 BC. First mentioned in funerary papyri, this particular tit amulet first appeared on Egyptian mummies in the mid-Eighteenth dynasty (1550 to 1295 BC).

Red Jasper is a stone that serves to strengthen and stabilize the Root chakra (that which is connected to one's survival, security and basic human potentiality), allowing one to feel grounded, thereby strengthening one's connection to Mother Earth. Perhaps this is why it was also favored by Indigenous peoples.

I find this to be a most comforting stone, probably because I have always needed to feel grounded and connected. When I feel grounded, I am calm. I feel soothed, almost as if a balm has been applied to my physical being.

Healing the Planet and Ourselves

It is important to follow your dreams, believing in yourself enough to see them realized. Dreams often represent the intuitive side of yourselves. You are a powerful creator, although you may not believe this to be so. All of creation began with thought and so it is thought that creates.

You must learn to think for yourselves, trusting the you that resides within. Do not act as many of the multitude in giving away this ability to think and create for yourselves.

Allow yourselves to experience life to the fullest. Even in situations that may seem dire, there is always a lesson to be learned. In the acceptance of such, one is able to move beyond the current situation to the next that comes your way. There will always be a new lesson to learn and experience.

There is much truth to the saying – inside every dark cloud there can be found a silver lining.

As one learns to embrace and accept the current situation, learning from it that which is needed, without judgment, one is able to gradually move on.

Healing the Planet and Ourselves

Pay close attention to the synchronicities that abound, for they are important signs from the heavens. They are to be seen as indications that you are on your path, one that you established for yourself. While each path may be different, for the lessons that you are to learn are not necessarily the lessons of another, be assured that each path leads back to the same: the divinity of self.

Life is not meant to be a struggle. Truth be told, the only battle that you must fight, and ultimately win, is the one that exists within.

Remain focused and centered on the beauty that exists within all situations and within all beings. Know that you continue to learn something valid, something new, each day.

Embrace this newness with the eagerness of a child, allowing the day to unfold as it shall.

Detach from the negative elements that serve to control your thoughts, words, deeds, actions, emotions. You must learn to remain true to the wonder of you.

Healing the Planet and Ourselves

Focus not on materialism, greed, revenge; these do not service the authentic self. Instead, become peace, love, forgiveness, compassion, nonjudgment, applying all, first and foremost, to yourselves.

It is important that each feel their connection to Mother Earth. This can be achieved by grounding.

We are here to assist you in this regard. In having made this connection, even within the vastness of this remarkable universe, you will not feel alone.

You will begin to understand what living in the now is all about.

While you have today, how you live today, via thought, word, deed, action and emotion, can significantly impact your future.

You need not serve anyone other than yourself. In this, you will also come to understand that in remaining true to one's authentic self, such is also connected to the uplifting of others. In truth, you may never know the full impact of your being on another.

Healing the Planet and Ourselves

Peace is your destiny. As one is uplifted, so, too, are all positioned in that upliftment. Let this become your mantra

aka Seer

Green Tiger Chalcedony

As early as the Bronze Age, Chalcedony was in use in the Mediterranean region. Interestingly enough, hot wax would not stick to this stone type and so it was that Chalcedony was often used to make wax seal impressions. There are hundreds of different varieties of Chalcedony, many of which have gem uses.

Beauty is often stated as existing within the eye of the beholder, when, in reality, beauty is to be found everywhere and in all things. Even in those instances and/or situations which seem desolate and forlorn, beauty can be found hiding within the depth and fortitude of the human spirit. One merely has to search for the beauty.

So, too, are you (the soul) beautiful. The physical vehicle (human body) also radiates an inherent beauty, for it allows you to manifest through its very medium.

Is this not a wondrous gift that you have been given?

Healing the Planet and Ourselves

Why do you, then, desecrate it with negative thoughts, negative words, harmful substances and actions of ill repute?

Your body is your temple. Should you not expend the utmost care and energy into its maintenance and well-being?

We see the beauty and wonder of you. Why is it that you struggle so with this concept? Accept and embrace your beauty. Having been created in the image of the creator, how can you be anything other than a creation of beauty?

Take the time to behold the majestic and vivid colors, the decadent smells, the soothing and delightful sounds, the marvelous textures and tastes. There is so much beauty that surrounds you. Take the time to enjoy these aspects of your physical experience.

aka Tiger

Pink Petalite

Petalite was first discovered by a Brazilian scientist while on a trip to Sweden at the end of the 1700's. Given its pink color, Petalite is a stone that can be used to balance the Heart chakra.

In my experiences with Petalite, I have found this stone to be very powerful. It has the ability to calm and reassure me; so, too, do I feel contented.

This is a stone that enables me to experience heart based consciousness on a deep and intimate level. I feel as if I am tuned into my spiritual essence when working with Petalite. I feel more expansive. I am able to feel blissful within the stillness.

Be not afraid to step into your spiritual destiny, your life plan. As many have written, you are a spiritual being having a human experience. It is this very experience that allows for your continued and expanded growth as a spiritual being.

Healing the Planet and Ourselves

The most important thing to grasp is the importance of embracing your heart consciousness by living the dictates of the heart, speaking the dictates of the heart, feeling the dictates of the heart.

Doing what you know to be right shall always win over doing that which you think is right. Take the time to feel with your heart.

Before responding to any given situation, take a few moments to ground yourself. Closing your eyes, take a few deep breaths. If responding in love, compassion and understanding, know that the right words to say will come to you with ease.

As the Beatles sang so wonderfully, all you need is love.

aka Dharma

Libyan Desert Glass

Located in the Libyan desert, one of the remotest parts of the Egyptian Libyan frontier, this considerably ancient stone (form of tektite) is reputed to be at least 30 million years old. While the silica content of tektites can range anywhere from 70 to 80 percent, the silica content of Libyan Desert Glass (LDG), by comparison, is 98 percent.

Made of melted and refused sand, science has come up with at least 10 theories [4] to explain its origin. A most notable reference, it is this very stone, in the form of the yellow straw colored carved scarab, that sits in the center of the breastplate belonging to Pharaoh Tutankhamen.

I feel incredibly grounded when I hold this stone.

---

[4] Olsen, JohnW. and Underwood, James R. *Desert Glass: An Enigma* article located in the September/October 1979 issue (Volume 30, Number 5) of <u>Saudi Aramco World</u> bimonthly magazine. Retrieved July 24, 2010 located at
http://www.saudiaramcoworld.com/issue/197905/desert.glass-an.enigma.htm

Healing the Planet and Ourselves

Perhaps it has something to do with its noted age. I feel very calm; in control of my emotions. I am able to think things through more clearly.

The wisest thing you can do is to learn how to succeed within your dualistic reality.

Within this duality lies energies that you deem to be both positive and negative, with the ultimate goal being to learn how to greatly reduce the negative (thoughts, words, actions) in order to establish a truly positive (and spiritually higher) existence as demonstrated through such components as truth, wisdom, empathy, compassion, nonjudgment, cooperation and fairness.

There can be no truth without discernment. When one accepts blindly, is that truth or enslavement? In keeping, there can be no wisdom without truth. It is your place to grow wise, truthful and just.

Truth and justice are paramount to universal order. When they are lacking, chaos and destruction reign supreme.

Healing the Planet and Ourselves

Many believe knowledge to be power when, in actual fact, it is wisdom that begets power. It can be said, therefore, that knowledge is the path that leads to wisdom.

Just as a great many strive to ascend to the top of the mountain, the pinnacle of the highest wisdom in the land, so, too, does this refer to ascension (which can be said to be the raising of one's being from negative mind to positive consciousness).

Negative mind (demonstrated by way of greed, deceit, fear, ignorance, arrogance, jealousy, violence, conquest, oppression, injustice) is akin to the me, me, me state of existence.

By comparison, positive consciousness (demonstrated by truth, discernment, wisdom, justice, patience, empathy, integrity, compassion, generosity, optimism, cooperation, fairness, equity, peace) is where you must find yourselves.

Ascension has always been this simple.

Ascension means to grow wiser, to walk the path of truth and justice, thereby becoming more godlike.

Healing the Planet and Ourselves

It becomes one's journey to traverse the mountain in an effort to reach the top, thereby transforming to a higher intellect affiliated with the highest wisdom.

aka Inner Glow

Iolite

Iolite is a beautiful violet-blue stone. It seems that the ancient mariners (Vikings), using the strong pleochroism of this stone, were able to look through thin Iolite lenses (thin slices of the stone) in order to determine the exact position of the sun on overcast days, thereby navigating their way safely to the New World and back again. In its day, I guess you could have referred to this as a compass of sorts.

When I wish to meditate with my inner Self, I will often do so with this particular stone in hand. It has been said that Iolite blends normal conscious thinking with that of intuitive knowing. This is exactly the merger that one needs to experience while on their inner journey.

Nothing happens that has not been first preceded by thought, whether this be understood (known) or not. Your reality is the culmination (product) of both individual and collective desires.

Healing the Planet and Ourselves

It becomes a given, then, that countless thoughts intersect and interact, amalgamating on a day to day basis.

As an individual currently living on this planet, you are also responsible for that which has been termed the collective (group) mind.

The deeply negative quality of both your past and current reality is what has resulted in the current collective situation.

Given that thoughts and ideas can bring about change in the collective consciousness, so, too, are they representative of life (creation).

Any positive change within the individual, ergo, also serves to affect the collective in a positive way; hence, this must become your mission.

aka Inner Knowledge

Larimar

A form of blue Pectolite, Larimar can be used to activate the Throat chakra (linked to our ability to communicate). A stone connected with feminine energies, the reading that came through was so incredibly appropriate.

It is in feeling emotional strength and stability that one can speak from the heart. When in the presence of this majestic stone, I feel a deep sense of peace. The tension eases from my body, helping me to relax in a way that makes me feel as if I am floating, peacefully and safely, in the warmest of waters imaginable.

The sun gives light. Light is synonymous with truth. Light is synonymous with illumination.

In keeping with ancient Egyptian symbolism, Ma'at was representative of truth and justice. Anything affiliated with air, sky, sun and the heavens, like Nut, was likened to feminine wisdom, as in the term Sophia; hence, we refer to the sun as Grandmother.

Healing the Planet and Ourselves

By comparison, the moon, referred to as the left eye of Ra (Horus) became the dual opposite of the sun, for it is the moon that merely reflects light. Anything affiliated with both the earth and the underworld, like Geb, was accorded masculine characteristics; hence, we refer to the moon as Grandfather.

Remembering that the sun (Aten) was a feminine symbol, Akhenaten chose to have himself portrayed with feminine attributes. Likewise, Thoth was always illustrated with the head of a bird, symbolic of a feminine mindset. It is the feminine (Ma'at) that has always been associated with truth, justice and wisdom.

In summation, when you work together for a better existence, so shall it be.

As long as you continue to struggle (as per money, politics and religion), on both an individual (microcosm) as well as a collective (macrocosm) level, you keep adding to the ever increasing chaos and disorder.

Healing the Planet and Ourselves

Clearly, the path of truth and justice is the way to a more positive and harmonious existence for everyone and everything.

aka Larissa, aka Mar

Dominican Amber

Fossilized pine tree resin, dating between 30 and 60 million years ago, Amber has been fashioned into jewelry for thousands of years. During the Middle Ages, many rosaries were crafted from this material. Amber serves to activate the Solar Plexus chakra (related to personal power, creativity and all matters of spiritual growth).

Living in the northern hemisphere where sunshine can be rather lacking, especially throughout the winter months, I find that Amber gets me through many of the symptoms associated with Seasonal Affective Disorder (SAD); a piece of solidified sunlight, if you will.

If unable to get to a tree to help me feel grounded, all I need to do is carry a few pieces of Amber about with me. Truly, Amber is the fossilized lifeblood of these ancient ones.

Most people believe that they live but one life and then they die.

Healing the Planet and Ourselves

As a result, there exists a minimal appreciation, at best, to work towards the solidifying of a better future for the collective (the whole).

If you knew that you were going to reincarnate back into the exact mess, with no idea as to where, then would you not be intrinsically motivated to create a better future?

Time is not linear, but cyclic. This universe (creator) arises from, and is driven by, your thoughts and desires (creation).

What goes around, comes around is a saying that many of you are familiar with.

Likewise for be careful what you wish for.

Let it be known that there is much truth inherent in these very words.

Whether future experiences are positive or negative in nature depends on you, both as an individual as well as a member of the collective (the macrocosm, the whole, the bigger picture).

Healing the Planet and Ourselves

With several millennia of history as proof, you must not find yourself on the wrong path, for therein shall lie your destruction. Money, religion and politics continue to drive your species towards the brink of annihilation.

You have the power to break these negative patterns (chains) of ages past, much of which continues merely as a result of collective ignorance, be it through inaction (in allowing another to think and act on your behalf) and/or misdeed.

As goes the saying, those who choose to ignore history are doomed to repeat it. Ignoring the truth of the past will merely result in a repeating of the same. All change, therefore, can only begin with the individual.

Having lived through the darkest of times (the Middle Ages, the Inquisition, the Holocaust, World War I, World War II, the bombing of Hiroshima, the war in Vietnam, the Gulf war, the ongoing war in the Middle East), humanity has been given the insight to free itself, thereby leading to a new and positive beginning of truth, wisdom and justice for all.

Healing the Planet and Ourselves

You have the power to become Masters of your own destiny.

Chaos and disorder can only be eliminated when truth and justice prevail.

Bronzite

Bronzite is the gemology name for the common mineral Enstatite. It is said that the ancient Romans relied on this stone to protect them from mental illness.

The very color of this stone (chocolate brown with golden swirls that shimmer, making it most chatoyant) fills me with delight. I have just discovered it to be associated with the zodiac sign of Leo, my sign. Might this be the reason for the deep resonance that I feel with this stone?

When feeling lethargic and run down, I always reach for a piece of Bronzite. After a few moments, I begin to feel quite energized and rejuvenated. I find it to be a very high energy stone.

Your truth has nothing to do with the perceived truth, the media created truth. You must delve ever so much deeper than that. You must be willing to go beyond the lies and the fear to get to the core of what is your truth.

Healing the Planet and Ourselves

Are you willing to face such a journey, a journey of fortitude and determination, to see that which lies beyond the confines of the box?

You are not mind (one that can only see the microcosm), but consciousness (one that can see the bigger picture, the totality of all that is, the macrocosm). You are here, both to challenge and be challenged. Do not accept blindly.

Seek the stillness that resides within, for there it is that you shall find your truth; the truth that has always been and always will be. Remaining true to this inherent truth is akin to walking the talk.

Listen to your heart by doing what you know is right (by intuiting, by feeling) and not that which you think is right (by rationalizing).

Do not blindly embrace the truth of another. Listen to what your heart tells you, for your heart will never steer you wrong.

You are a being of compassion. Compassion is the way back to a peaceful life.

Healing the Planet and Ourselves

As within the eye of the hurricane, there can be found a calmness, a stillness, a peace; so, too, will you find the same within your being. You just have to get there.

aka Solomon

Septarian

Septarian nodules were formed during the Cretaceous period, 50 to 70 million years ago, when the Gulf of Mexico reached what is now known as southern Utah (USA).

Decomposing sea creatures, killed by volcanic eruptions, and the resulting climatic catastrophes, had a chemical attraction for the sediment around them, forming mud balls. As the ocean receded, these mud balls were left to dry and crack in extreme conditions. Their chemical composition allowed them to shrink at the same time, trapping the cracks inside.

As decomposed Calcite from the shells of the sea creatures was carried into the cracks of these mud balls, Calcite crystals formed. A thin wall of Calcite was transformed into Aragonite, separating the heavy clay exteriors from the Calcite centres. These are very energetically potent stones, possessing the energies of Yellow Calcite, Brown Aragonite, White (Clear) Barite and Grey Limestone.

Healing the Planet and Ourselves

When I am working with this stone, I feel highly energized. Joyful and optimistic, I feel connected to Mother Earth in such a way that it is a most reassuring feeling.

I find it quite intriguing that I am always drawn to ancient stones as well as fossils. Might this be because their energies remember a time when the earth and her inhabitants were not experiencing what we are now? Might they remember a time of peace, a time of equity, a time of cooperation and optimism? Could it be that I also lived upon the earth during such times? To my mind, all is possible.

The wonder of life.

The wonder of creation.

We are amazed by the free will that continues to create. Thoughts, you see, are so incredibly powerful.

Although you are moulded by past experience(s), who you are today is not who you were ten, or even fifteen, years ago.

Healing the Planet and Ourselves

You are forever changing, forever evolving, forever Becoming. Do not be disturbed by this. Change (evolution) is of significant importance.

To know what you want, to know what you do not want; both are imperative to your Becoming (that which you have always been).

Embrace this newness with the wonderment of a child, knowing that what you experience today (via belief systems and upheld truths) will differ from that of tomorrow.

Therein lies the freshness of each new day that must be embraced and lived to the fullest.

aka Septaria

Calavera Stone

Calavera is a druzy kissed stone that comes to us from the state of Wyoming (USA), where it is mined on a very limited basis, on the edge of a precipice, which prevents any major mining scale from occurring. Interestingly, the word *calavera* is spanish for skull.

According to Ravenia Youngman of Crystal Skull Head Quarters, [5] an online eBay store, Calavera Stone is also known as the *Stone of Primal Memories* in that it can assist one on their meditative travels to the far reaches of the memories of the soul.

In working with this stone, I feel connected to that which is larger than my physical being, making me feel completely expansive in spirit.

Seek ye (knowledge) so that ye shall find (knowledge), for in this search ye shall find truth, wisdom and justice; all of which constitute more than mere knowledge.

---

[5] http://stores.ebay.ca/Crystal-Skull-Head-Quarters

Healing the Planet and Ourselves

Each of these individual components must first be applied to the inner self so that you can model such to the outer world.

This outside world mirrors that which your inner world chooses to embody, to believe, to present.

Everything starts with you as an individual. This is a most fundamental premise because you can only change one person: yourself.

As people become witness to the energetic and vibrational changes, you become a model of possibility to them so that they, too, might be brave enough to follow in your footsteps.

This is a materialization of monumental importance.

You must learn to embody that which you want to see more of in the outer world, be it peace, love, forgiveness, compassion, truth, nonjudgment, patience, integrity, cooperation, generosity.

It is in the changing of one's self that change also becomes possible, feasible, imminent, within the overall collective.

Healing the Planet and Ourselves

By your example, so, too, shall you encourage others to do the same.

Life is so very precious. You have been given a wondrous gift. The time to awaken is now, but you must be willing to escape the Matrix in order to do so.

You are more powerful that you can ever begin to imagine. You just have to remember.

aka Memories

Star Rose Quartz

The only difference between Rose Quartz and Star Rose Quartz is that the latter delineates an asterism (a six sided star pattern) when illuminated by a point-like light source. In addition, Star Rose Quartz is only found in a few locations around the world.

Rose Quartz is the stone to reach for when love (of yourself, your partner, your children, family, friends, the Earth, the universe) is paramount. If we are to graduate from a reality of fear to a reality of love, this is the very stone we need to be spending time with. Given its pink color, Rose Quartz is a stone that can be used to balance the Heart chakra. This stone will serve to assist you on your journey to heart based consciousness (compassion, empathy), which is who we really are.

When the Beatles sang all you need is love, did you not resonate with those lyrics?

Healing the Planet and Ourselves

In truth, these words are far more important than a great many of you will ever come to realize.

There is nothing you can do that can't be done: you are your own creator. What is it that you wish to create for yourself? On the flip side, what is it that you wish to uncreate?

Nothing you can do, but you can learn how to be you in time: you are an infinite and divine being of limitless compassion.

There is nothing you can know that isn't known: seek ye knowledge, wisdom and justice, so that ye may find (all of these) and know the truth.

Nothing you can see that isn't shown: by having the eyes to see outside the confines of the box (Matrix).

Nowhere you can be that isn't where you're meant to be: you choose those experiences that aid in your continual evolvement.

Whilst created in love, many of you do not love the divine and wondrous beings that you are.

Healing the Planet and Ourselves

You must get back to acknowledgment and acceptance of the self (both light and dark aspects) so that you can learn to love the totality of your being.

Now is the time to come back to the real you: a being of love, a being of compassion, a creator of importance.

Learning to love the totality of your being equates to the healing of the psyche, for it is only fear that holds you back. Working your way through the fear takes everything you have, and yet it is necessary.

Love is the answer.

Humans are afraid of a great many things: relationships, intimacy, living, dying, social rejection, heights, spiders, snakes, terrorist attacks, war, the future, being alone, nuclear war, flying, public speaking, the dark, failure, commitment, driving, dogs, dentists, needles, water, abandonment, clowns, falling, change, germs, crowds, being touched, open spaces, closed spaces, thunder.

In truth, we could go on and on and on and on.

Healing the Planet and Ourselves

It is essential that each of you learn to become more trusting of your intuitive self, of your knowing self, for this is merely the beginning back to completeness.

Love is the answer.

You are here because you wanted to be here. You are here because you wanted this specific experience. You are here to find the peace (stillness, bliss) within. If you are able to find the beauty within, despite the dark and forlorn experiences, you will have succeeded in your mission.

Love is the answer.

If you can remain calm amidst the fear and chaos that abounds, you will have succeeded in your mission.

Love is the answer.

If you can learn to replace all of the negative thoughts, words and actions with positive, caring and compassionate alternatives, you will have succeeded in your mission.

Love is the answer.

Healing the Planet and Ourselves

If you are able to remember and re-connect with who you are, an infinite being of divine light, you will have succeeded in your mission.

Love is the answer.

Take the time to embrace the beauty and wonderment of you.

aka Aquarius

Green Grossular Garnet

While most believe Garnet to be red in color, there are actually many different types of Garnet, each with their own color compositions. Rhodolite, Almandine, Spessartine, Grossular, Andradite and Uvarovite all belong to the Garnet group of minerals.

Having been used since the Bronze Age, as both gemstones and abrasives, one of the most sought after varieties of gem Garnet is the fine green grossular garnet also called Tsavorite.

When I feel particularly challenged, this is the stone that I reach for. In working with the energies of Grossular Garnet, I feel an exuberant sense of optimism. Might that be related to the fact that this stone is noted as being the stone of confidence and stability?

What is reality? Indeed, this is a most fascinating question.

Does anyone really know?

Healing the Planet and Ourselves

Given that there are limitless perceptions of this reality of yours, so, too, are there limitless realities and limitless possibilities, even though it fully appears that all of you are sharing the same reality.

This clearly means that you can choose to create a reality of your making.

Will it be one based on fear, chaos and destruction? Will it be one based on compassion, nonjudgment and nurturance?

All exists within the realm of possibility. You need but ask of yourselves: what is it that I wish to create?

In placing your complete and deliberate attention (thoughts, words, energy) on something, you are creating a future as decided by you. What this also means is that the future of 2012 is one that you are able to create for yourself.

Did you not know that in choosing, you are always creating?

What, then, is it that you are wanting to create?

Healing the Planet and Ourselves

Indeed, this is a most exciting and transformative epoch in which to have returned.

We take the time to applaud all of you in your desire to incarnate in these most arduous of times.

Coming from love, coming from heart consciousness, all else falls into place. Believing in the strength and optimism of the human spirit, we know you are more than up to the challenge.

aka The Optimist

Smoky Quartz with Black Tourmaline

This particular piece (a collector's item with four natural double terminated Smoky Quartz crystals, complete with Black Tourmaline inclusions) is one of my all time favorites.

Smoky Quartz is one of my intimate grounding stones. It serves to assist me in feeling present within my physical world. It also allows me to feel deeply connected with Mother Earth.

Black Tourmaline, also known as Schorl, is denoted as being the stone to assist in psychic protection, especially if you work and/or live in challenging places or situations.

In having acquired a majestic piece with the properties of both, each serves to enhance the other.

Double terminated crystals have terminations (points) at each end of the crystal. It is believed that they have the ability to both receive and transmit energies.

It is for this reason that DT crystals are of significant importance to those who are involved with healing work (as in Reiki) for themselves and/or others. I can attest to the fact that they certainly *strengthen* the flow of energy during my long distance Reiki energy sends.

You must work, in earnest, towards becoming completely centered at the emotional level, for this is what shall enable you to be able to detach from the response(s) created, courtesy of one's uncontrolled emotion(s) such as fear and distrust. You must not allow yourselves to be ruled by your emotions.

Thoughts, words and deeds based upon unruly and haphazard emotion, all serve to further embroil one until they are no longer able to think coherently. In fact, this usually results in complete inaction, an emotional based response that encourages people to shut down and give their power away.

After all, is it not easier to have someone else think, respond, and make decisions for you amidst the reigning chaos?

Healing the Planet and Ourselves

It is imperative that you achieve calmness, balance and harmony.

As you reach and adhere to these mental states of being on the inside, so, too, are they reflected in your outer physical world; in addition, this further serves to create the reality of your choosing.

Live the reality of your choice to the fullest.

Embrace the wonder of each new day.

Spend time reconnecting with nature.

Take the time to exercise your physical body, feeling the strength, determination and perseverance that results.

Prepare simple, yet wholesome, meals to enjoy, losing yourself in the smells, colors, textures and tastes.

Spend time in meditation and blissful stillness.

Read to expand your knowledge.

Question that which the multitude believes.

Healing the Planet and Ourselves

Seek that which resonates with you.

Be not afraid to think outside the box in your endeavor to ascertain that which outlines your truth(s).

Be of service to others, without neglecting yourself.

Do all that you can to assist Mother Earth (in your concentrated efforts to reduce, reuse, and recycle).

Feel the inherent pleasure that comes from activities such as those outlined above, becoming a living example to friends, family, acquaintances. It may be that you are able to inspire others to do the same.

Feel the contentment that comes from having lived a full day in reverence to the Creator.

Feel the joie de vivre from living the experience as it is meant to be lived, as only one, such as yourself, can live it.

Only you can make the choice to do so.

Lemurian Seed Crystals

Lemurian Seed Crystals are a special variety of clear Quartz crystals that have been found in the Diamantina region of Brazil. These crystals display some very unique ladder like groove markings.

Many individuals, myself included, are drawn to the fabled land of Lemuria; an ancient civilization also known as Mu (meaning the Motherland), believed to have sunk beneath the Pacific Ocean thousands of years ago. In fact, it is said that the volcanoes of Hawaii, as well as other Polynesian islands, are, in fact, the tops of ancient Lemurian mountains.

Lemuria has been touted as a civilization whereby one felt in touch with the Divine as well as the totality of all life; the very same spiritual consciousness that many are striving for today.

Could it be that Lemuria was the basis for the Garden of Eden, making this a very real place?

Healing the Planet and Ourselves

It has been said that these particular crystals are encoded with the vibrations of Lemurian consciousness; a consciousness that was based upon heart connection with Spirit. It can easily be concluded, therefore, that the Lemurians were emotionally centered individuals with a strong spiritual consciousness.

When working with these crystals in meditation, I feel more whole as a person. I also feel balanced (physical, mental, emotional, spiritual) on all levels. While the energies may be soft and loving, feminine in nature, they are also intensely powerful. I enjoy working with these specialty crystals when conducting long distance Reiki energy sends.

A caretaker to numerous Lemurian Seed Crystals, I chose to meditate with the very first being that came to live with me.

We are addressing you, Starwalker, for you, too, have come from the stars. You are the very essence of the universe, comprised of the same stardust as all of creation.

Reaching for, achieving and attaining, the quiet within is what replenishes the well.

Healing the Planet and Ourselves

The challenge, especially in these times, lies in finding the time and space in which to reach this knowing state, and yet it is imperative that you do so.

You must take the time out of your hectic, fast paced, stressful lives (of your own creation) in order to do so. Life is simply what you make it.

In your stargazing on a clear night, have you ever wondered from whence you came from before braving it all to travel to the faculty of earth? Everyone knows that earth is the school that most elect to enroll in, knowing, full well, that one's experience here is not always an easy one. That is why you committed yourself to coming and we hereby salute you.

If it is your wish to recreate the Garden of Eden prototype within your current existence, you must begin by reclaiming your power, by thinking and responding for yourselves.

You must be willing to step away from the herd in order to start thinking outside the box (pen), for this has served to enslave you to a power that exists outside of yourselves.

Healing the Planet and Ourselves

Might it be that this original enslavement was what you have termed the fall from grace?

Stand tall. Stand firm in what you believe, knowing that you are on the road to remembrance. Graduating from an ego based consciousness to a heart centered consciousness shall become your earned degree. It is up to you to reconnect with, and start remembering, that which has long been forgotten.

There was a time when peace enveloped the entirety of this planet; a time of considerable spiritual consciousness. Some of you may actually remember the time of this past golden age. So, too, is there to be another time when peace shall reign supreme once more, and that time is now.

Do not allow another to create your reality for you. It is up to you to create that which you envision for yourself.

Believe. Act according to the dictates of your heart. Give thanks for the denoted outcome.

We are but here to assist, as crystalline midwives, in its birthing. As you will it, so shall it be.

Spider Jasper

As one continues throughout the course of this text, they will discover that I am very much drawn to the stone type Jasper, of which there are many different varieties; there are so many, that I no longer endeavor to keep count. Instead, I simply focus on those which beckon to me, of which this stone is but one.

As spiders weave their delicate, intricate and beautiful webs, so do the lattice-like lines, usually red in color, on this predominantly black stone, remind me of the same. I find that I am quite mesmerized by the strength of the beauty inherent within this stone.

Spider Jasper, also known as Stormking Jasper, is, like its Red Jasper counterpart, a stone that serves to strengthen and stabilize the Root chakra (that which is connected to one's survival, security and basic human potentiality), allowing one to feel grounded (which leads to further strengthening of one's connection to Mother Earth).

Healing the Planet and Ourselves

This stone is only found in the state of Idaho (USA). I feel very comforted by the presence of this stone; so much so, in fact, that I want to continue holding it for extended periods of time. To me, Spider Jasper feels like a stone for the enlightenment warrior.

A storm is brewing; a storm unlike any that you may have witnessed and/or experienced before, for it is one that you must engage – a storm (battle) of the mind.

The battlefield of the mind is merely the war that plays out between dark and light, a battle that everyone must conquer. Such is the journey of every human soul, the pathless journey towards self-realization, a journey in consciousness, a journey in metamorphosis. It is also the quest for self-transformation, the journey of an observer, the journey to freedom.

At some point, this is a journey that all will take. One cannot be filled and directed by both darkness (ego) and light (mindfulness, awareness, transcendence) at the same time.

Healing the Planet and Ourselves

There is a choice that must be made, with one of these facets taking over the helm of the mind.

You are invited to fight in a war like no other; a war where loss is actually counted as gain, a war where surrender can only be viewed as victory, a war where the enemy you must face, an enemy of unimaginable superiority, is none other than yourself.

You must become the operative, ready to engage in a battle against one's self; the battle of which is to secure the existence of the authentic self.

Time stands for no man. Are you ready to begin?

aka Storm

Labradorite

Labradorite always makes me think of transformation and Merlin, the Druid-like wizard associated with Arthurian lore. Some of the more prominent Merlin figures of today are teachers and mentors, such as Obi-Wan Kenobi (Star Wars), Gandalf the White (The Lord of the Rings) and Albus Dumbledore (Harry Potter). Generally speaking, however, Merlin is viewed as an Ancient who possessed superior knowledge of the universe; someone from whom we can all learn something.

Labradorite, so named because it was first discovered in Labrador, Canada, is a fascinatingly beautiful mineral, one that is known for its remarkable vivid flashes of blue, violet, green, yellow and orange (dubbed, most aptly, labradorescence). Labradorites found in Finland are called Spectrolite. Larvikite is the name that has been given to silvery gray Labradorites located in Scandinavia. Another close cousin to Labradorite is Nuummite, a gemstone native to Greenland.

Healing the Planet and Ourselves

Living on the west coast of Newfoundland, just a hop, skip and a jump from the Labrador coast, I feel an incredible affinity with this stone. Each time I place a piece in my left hand, my palm begins to tingle. I can actually begin to feel the energy coursing through my body.

A champion of the underdog, this is an incredibly powerful and protective stone.

Did you not know that there is a Merlin that exists within yourselves?

Did you not know that everything that you will ever need already exists within?

Having entered the portal to earth, courtesy of your birth parents, the Veil of Forgetting is immediate.

Having already decided on much of the blueprint for your current life, when you experience resonance with something, it may result in goosebumps arising on the flesh of your skin, an immediate reaction. Make note of such happenings, for your truth is to be found within.

Healing the Planet and Ourselves

By the same token, when you experience synchronicities (as in the right book finds you; you are thinking about someone and they reach you, be it by way of email or telephone; you are thinking about a specific situation and a pertinent song comes over the airwaves; you have put forth a question to the universe and a bird crosses your path, directly in front of you), pay attention for these are messages (signposts) that cannot be ignored.

All are to help you remember the totality of who they are.

You elected to come to this reality for the diversification of the experience, whereby all serve to expand, and enhance, your essence (spiritual being). As you change (evolve), so, too, does all of creation, including the Prime Creator (who lives vicariously through your own experience).

This is why we refer to it as a state of Becoming.

How fast or slow you get there becomes your choice. While there are many individual paths back to Source, all eventually arrive at the same destination.

Healing the Planet and Ourselves

As you become willing to explore, to challenge, to dissect, the Veil of Forgetting begins to thin, allowing you to fully embrace the fact that you are a spiritual being immersed within a human experience.

All experiences are unique to the individual experiencing them; this is what makes the ride so fascinating. You are cautioned, however, to refrain from becoming so enmeshed that you believe the experience to be real.

There is but a single choice to be made (fear versus love) when creating with consciousness.

As long as one creates out of fear, one is controlled by the ego.

The moment one creates out of love, they are truly free.

All of this plays a significant part in the state of Becoming.

Illusions can only control you when you think they are real. Be not afraid to embrace that which you know to be real.

aka Stargate

Ametrine

The major world producer of Ametrine is the Anahi Mine in Bolivia. This mine became famous in the seventeenth century when a Spanish conquistador received it as part of a dowry for marrying a princess named Anahi from the Ayoreos tribe. Ametrine was then introduced to Europe, through gifts from the conquistador, to the Spanish queen.

Ametrine is a delightful combination of Amethyst and Citrine. I find the blending of purples (Amethyst) with golden yellow hues (Citrine) most appealing. They are soothing and calming (Amethyst) as well as purifying and energizing (Citrine).

I feel both a sense of rightness as well as a sense of peace and contentment (relaxation) when working with this stone. Likewise, there is sense of companionship that abounds.

A blending of two precious stones, so, too, are you a blending of the spiritual and the physical. This also serves to highlight the duality that exists regarding your planet.

Healing the Planet and Ourselves

If it were not for the duality that exists, how would you know what you did not want? In order to focus on that which you want, you need also know what it is that you do not want; hence, the importance for what may appear to be a paradox.

When the two become as one, when the dualistic parts of the self (light and dark, love and hate, masculine and feminine) have been integrated, you revert back to your truest nature: one of compassion and compassionate allowing. The self is balanced.

Every time you are at peace, so, too, are you enlightened. Inner peace is what must be attained. In this experience, you are happy and content, connected to the Source.

You must depart from inner turmoil as this is what suffocates your spirit, preventing you from living from your higher self.

Enlightenment is a state of being whereby you are reunited with your true spiritual self. Indeed, this is what is meant by the words Holy Grail.

Healing the Planet and Ourselves

It is this connectedness (this freedom of the self) that leads one to the ultimate and definitive realization that all is one. When you realize that all is connected, you are able to joyfully accept and live life as per your creation.

In the words of our brother, Yeshua ben Yosef ... "Seek ye knowledge and ye shall find the truth that liberates. Seek ye discipline in the persisting with positive thoughts. Seek ye the joy of creating, the joy of learning, the joy of experiencing. Seek ye the realm of infinite possibilities for therein ye shall find the all. Seek ye the seer that ye be." [6]

The balancing of the physical (energies, emotions) with the spiritual (inner peace, harmony) results in manifested physical attributes such as: less stress; less anxiety; increased happiness; increased health and wellness; youthful exuberance; youthful looks; more energized; increased positivity; increased longevity and increased productivity in the workplace – all of which serve to raise one's vibrational levels.

---

[6] Doucette, Michele. (2010) <u>Veracity At Its Best</u> (p 141). McMinnville, TN: St. Clair Publications.

Healing the Planet and Ourselves

Take the time to enjoy life.

Take the time to experience living in the now.

Golden C

Golden C belongs to the Spodumene family, which also includes Kunzite, Hiddenite and Tryphane. As per the Lithium Based Stones chapter located towards the end of the book, the Golden C crystal, an extremely rare stone mined near San Diego, California, at the turn of the 20th century, contains upwards of 35% Lithium. This crystal also contains both Gallium and Beryllium, making its crystalline structure very different from that of the other crystals in the Spodumene family.

In accordance with a San Jose, California, newspaper clipping of 1982 ... "Gallium is a very rare substance. It is neither metal nor non-metal. It is so rare that a three-inch wafer costs about $300 compared to $5 for a slice of silicon (quartz crystal). The secret of gallium's speed is what chemists call its 'high electron mobility'. At a given voltage, gallium's electrons move seven times faster than those of silicon (quartz crystal). At its highest speed, gallium chips don't overheat or self-destruct as silicon chips do. More importantly, gallium chips only require 1% of the power that is required by a silicon chip." [7]

In keeping with further elemental analysis, as per the same website, Golden C is similar in properties to Coenzyme Q-10, which is an essential nutrient for healthy body cells.

As soon as this crystal is positioned in my left hand, the palm begins to tingle. I am able to feel an immediate denseness when, in actual fact, the crystals themselves are extraordinarily light.

Mere moments later, the vibration actually begins to feel like a steady heart beat. I am immediately drawn to the heart of the Great Mother: Gaia (our planet).

It is important to know that every crystal responds in a different fashion, which is why tuning into the energies of the crystals is so very important.

When visiting this crystal, I feel so free.

---

[7] *Crystal Structured Water* article. Retrieved on August 3, 2010 at http://www.luminanti.com/goldenc.html

Healing the Planet and Ourselves

I feel completely plugged into my higher self. I feel light, and yet am also able to experience a denseness in the palm of my hand, a paradox if you will; a merger of two important components that are almost comparable to a lightness of body within the physical frame; a merger of spiritual with physical.

I also experience continued resonance in the form of goosebumps. Knowing this to be a personal sign of my inner truth, I take the time to pay close attention.

As Trooper sang ... If you don't like what you've got, why don't you change it. Only you have the power to change what it is that you do not like.

In continuation of the same ... If your world is all screwed up, rearrange it. Going from the negative (thoughts, words, actions) to the positive is one way in which to rearrange things in the outer physical world, is it not?

Positivity is foremost. Not only does it serve to keep your physical vehicle healthy, it also assists in your spiritual evolution as well.

Healing the Planet and Ourselves

It is imperative that you develop, and maintain, a clear vision of what you want in your world, for only then will you become enveloped with feelings of inner peace and total well-being.

A deep sense of connection is so very important. We can help provide the spiritual association of which you seek.

Rainbow Mayanite Quartz

This new variety of Quartz has been found in the foothills of the Cascade Mountains in Eastern Washington state (USA). Rainbow Mayanite Quartz is a natural gemstone said to be a special crystal to assist one through the planetary transition of December 2012, as predicted by the Mayan peoples.

Similar in color to crystals by the name of Golden Healer, there is something majestic about them in that they also demonstrate flashes of color associated with the rainbow.

Almost immediately, when positioned in my left hand, my palm begins to vibrate very strongly, almost as if a heartbeat existed within this very crystal itself.

I am able to detect an incredible warm energy, one of strength and reassurance, from this stone, becoming awash with a feeling that all is well. Without making an attempt to meditate, this piece allows me to easily drift off to the stillness within.

Healing the Planet and Ourselves

A new find, there is nothing written as to these particular crystals. Individuals must therefore intuit, on their own, what it is that these crystals have to share with them.

Newbies to you because we are a relatively new find, in truth, we have existed for eons.

It is quite fitting that we are being 'discovered' in this current time.

Only you, in your meditative efforts, can determine how we are to assist you in keeping with the upcoming transitional cosmic event of 2012 and beyond.

Ajoite

A rare mineral, Ajoite is frequently seen as an inclusion in Quartz. My pieces (in their natural, rough, state) originated from the Messina Cooper Mine in Messina, South Africa, with the Ajoite being a majestic teal green.

When working with this stone, I feel a deep sense of feminine energies, especially those that revolve around truth, wisdom, justice and compassion. I also feel very nurtured when meditating with this stone, the energy being a soft and loving one. At the same time, I also find myself feeling uplifted. Due to its calming effect on the emotional body, I have read that it is a most effective stone to use when PMS or menopausal symptoms are the cause of one's mood swings.

We come to you in love, knowing that we can assist you in reaching a spiritual expanse. While we belong to the Great Mother, we have agreed to become tools of transformation for the evolution of humanity.

Healing the Planet and Ourselves

Like the workings of a portal, we can conduct a transference of frequencies.

Words are likes bytes of wisdom, should you wish to avail of them as such. Many of you may find this avenue of ours somewhat strange, but rest assured, we are speaking through this individual.

We hope that many of you will elect to work with us. We have much to share.

To work for the highest good of all is our noteworthy aim.

Dragon's Blood Granite

Dragon's Blood Granite is also known as Champagne Granite. When working with this stone, I feel the oneness that abounds. I feel peace and contentedness. This is a very soothing energy to work with.

Ancient cultures had various ideas about the nature of infinity. The symbol for infinity is sometimes called the lemniscate. It comes from the latin word *lemniscus* which means ribbon (∞). With no beginning and no end, meaning an unboundedness, it looks like the numeral eight on its side. Is one's inner search naught but the search for themselves; a search that also encompasses infinity?

Ah, yes ...... infinity. You have such incredible difficulty with this concept for, in truth, it is far beyond anything that your 3D minds can logically comprehend.

You are quite right when you say there is no beginning and no end.

Healing the Planet and Ourselves

Instead, there exists endless, ceaseless, continual, infinite and unlimited creation. Is this not consistent with the numeral pi (π) that goes on unto forever, ad infinitum?

You are very much your own creator, whether you realize this to be true or not. For those who acknowledge this, they must believe in both creator and creation, lest they revert to creating by default (which is merely the unconscious act of creation).

There is much empowerment in knowing that you are responsible for that which you create; so, too, is there freedom in this knowledge.

All is energy. All is vibration. How, then, does one create?

They create via their thoughts, words and actions, all of which are sending out vibrational frequencies that serve to attract more of the same. The real challenge, however, lies in learning how to remain detached in your creating.

What do we mean by this?

Healing the Planet and Ourselves

Buddha once said that attachment leads to suffering. These are most wise words that we are taking the time to share with you.

In remaining attached to thoughts, feelings, objects and people, you will, at some point, come to the realization that these attachments are primarily based on fear, lack and/or worthlessness.

Take the time to think about what this has to say about you.

When you choose to live from an avenue of love, trust and self-worth, you come to understand further that you are detached from your goal(s), living in trust. This does not mean that you give up your intention to create, that you give up your desire. In essence, this means that you are allowing the universe to bring it to you.

Attachment actually leads to the blocking of one's energy and positive vibrational flow. When you are completely attached to something, there is a physical hook that is created; so much so, that you actually feel considerable tension affiliated with your attachment.

Healing the Planet and Ourselves

When your happiness depends on something outside of yourself, be that a thought, a feeling, a physical event, you become a slave to your dependent attachment. One is merely existing, and not living, as a result.

The ego believes that success only comes from having attained a certain outcome.

When one is connected to their inner being, their Higher Self, this is never the case. As long as one continues to struggle, one is never able to appreciate the fact that infinite power exists within.

Truly, you do not need to work so hard. You must learn to become more trusting of the universe. You must learn to release any thought, any feeling, any memory, that serves to keep you attached to the suffering that ensues.

In the words of Sheryl Crow, a singer/songwriter of your time ... it is not about getting what you want; it is about wanting what you've got.

aka Infinity

Petrified Peanut Wood

Petrified Peanut Wood, also known as Australian Opalite Conifer, as well as Teredo Wood, is a rare type of petrified wood (Araucaria species) found in the Kennedy Ranges of Western Australia. These trees grew 70 million years ago in the noted Cretaceous period.

Peanut Wood refers not to a type of tree, but to the appearance of the peanut shaped, light color, markings against the black background of this petrified wood. Peanut Wood was created from wood that washed into the ocean and became infested with small marine clams (Teredo Mullusks, also known as shipworms) that bore into the wood. Sinking to the bottom of the ocean floor, the bore holes filled with radiolarite, and the wood later petrified.

When working with this stone, I am reminded to live by both my truths as well as my ideals. I love the glossy sheen of this fossil when it is polished.

Healing the Planet and Ourselves

As soon as you stop judging, both yourself and others, accepting what is, you experience a complete liberation from the mind (ego). This is the very freedom and inner peace sought by all; a freedom that comes from detachment.

One has not the need to defend. One has not the need to protect. There is no good. There is no bad. All, in truth, is orchestrated by the divinity that exists within your very selves.

What you focus on, is what you become: peace, love, forgiveness, compassion, nonjudgment, harmlessness, enlightenment, liberation. He who is content with what he has, is the richest of men.

Opposites exist merely to complement each other. This is what is meant by duality.

When you are able to free your mind from both aspects, you are able to reside within the polarity without actually being part of it. Your entire reality then shifts into a different dimension, if you will.

Healing the Planet and Ourselves

All experiences are pertinent. All experiences are necessary for personal growth and expansion. To become more aware, more conscious, in keeping with each experience, this is why you are here.

To comprehend that in harming another, so, too, are you harming yourself is a most challenging concept for many to understand.

You, alone, are the master of your mind. The mind (consciousness) lies at the very heart of your physical temple.

The moment you see that we are all connected, that we are all one, the search for enlightenment is over.

aka Patience

Sonora Sunrise

Sonora Sunrise, a relatively new discovery from Mexico, is the name given to a combination of copper minerals: Chrysocolla, which is a beautiful turquoise blue color, and Cuprite, which has some fantastic red variations. For the many who are able to attest to the healing quality of copper bracelets, so, too, is this stone a natural healer.

I like to surround myself with copper based stones due to the difficulties that I have with my legs. Copper based stones provide physical relief to persons diagnosed with arthritis and rheumatoid arthritis. I can certainly attest to a former student, diagnosed as having rheumatoid arthritis in Grade 1, who swore by her copper bracelet.

Do you remember going to the park as a child? When you were on the swing, you always wanted to go higher and higher. Riding the teeter totter was always an adventure; up, down, up, down, up, down. So, too, must the pendulum swing.

Healing the Planet and Ourselves

Life is but a lesson, always teaching you what you need to know. There may be negative experiences, so that one is able to learn how to surrender to the experience by letting go and letting God. There may be positive experiences, so that one can experience the sacredness, the oneness, the interconnectedness, of all life.

Can you see, then, how experiences, therefore, are neither good nor bad, but merely there for you to learn from?

Too often, however, life appears rife with problems; hence, the eternal swing, back and forth, back and forth, back and forth; never, it seems, residing in one arena.

These so-called problems cannot be solved by changing one's outer (physical) world.

Instead, they can only be changed by the shifting of one's inner (spiritual) world whereby they are viewed as blessings and opportunities in camouflage.

Healing the Planet and Ourselves

The lesson you are here to learn is how to balance the highs and the lows, both of which are extremes, so that you are able to co-exist with such experiences, seeing beyond both levels.

As you continue to watch the pendulum, without engaging the mind, you will become more of a detached observer.

It is this increased awareness, this mindfulness, this relaxed state (where one reacts without judgment) that allows you to reach your natural enlightened state, for therein lies your new found freedom.

aka Freedom

Nuummite

Stated to be the oldest mineral in existence, Nuummite is found in an area north of Nuuk (southern Greenland), an iron-ore region which dates back 4 billion years. Given that it is found in high, rugged, mountain terrain, such makes it difficult to obtain; hence, the high costs related to the stone itself.

The base color of the Nuummite can range from charcoal gray to black, with its iridescent colors including red, orange, gold, silver, yellow, green, blue and violet. Truly, this is a most majestic stone to behold.

I think of Nuummite as a stone for the creative sorceror; namely, ourselves. No doubt a stone utilized by the ancients before us: having identified it as the oldest living mineral in our world, to me, this speaks volumes. In working with this stone, one can be brought to see with their hearts, recognizing the inner strength and depth of spirit that is reflective within a calm state of mind.

Healing the Planet and Ourselves

Despite the small size of the Nuummite pieces that are in my care, there is an amazing density to them that makes the palm of my left hand feel incredibly heavy. The energetic vibration is a very steady (slow) feeling; one that makes me feel wonderfully grounded.

It has been shared that we are a mystical stone. Mysticism is but the pursuit of spiritual truth through direct experience and intuitive means.

Some may refer to this as [1] becoming aware of the nature of the self through both observation and detachment, [2] liberation from the cycles of karma, [3] an individual union with the Divine, [4] experiencing enlightenment, [5] experiencing divine consciousness, and [6] experiencing transcendence.

Clearly, these are words that refer to your experience of the vast and interconnected oneness of all life.

In working with us, you will become your own wizard, your own sorcerer, your own Merlin, if we may use these terms.

Healing the Planet and Ourselves

On your quest for self-mastery, we are the necessary stone of inner power. This means that you will undergo a deep journey to the core of the authentic self when working with us.

Several crystal companions have already shared that you are the master of your own mind. This must be believed, by you, for change to occur.

Change is of the utmost importance for it allows you to venture from one belief system, one level of truth, one individual paradigm, to another.

In truth, the only constant in life is change and yet many of you fear change. This need not be. Change allows all to Be (as they are) and to Become (who they truly are).

It is imperative that you learn to become nonjudgmental.

You must learn to disentangle yourself from emotionally charged situations that are governed by the ego. You must learn to disentangle yourself from the collective mindset of laws, rules and dogma. Superseding such will allow you to experience your own freedom and resolution.

Healing the Planet and Ourselves

Become mindful of who you Are and who you are Becoming.

Take the time to embrace the wonder and beauty of you as both creation and creator. Take full responsibility for that which is created by you, for this is what leads to complete and total empowerment.

The future is yours to see; que sera, sera.

aka Sorceror

Anorthosite

Anorthosite forms deep underground, and, while less abundant than basalt or granite, makes up about 60% of the earth's crust (also making it an extremely old stone, perhaps as old as Nuummite). Interestingly enough, Anorthosite was predominantly represented in rock samples brought back from the Moon.

In discovering that I am at least 4 billion years old, what does this tell you about Mother Earth? With regards to the planet itself, there is more to physical science than you are aware.

Take the time to feel the heart of the Great Mother. Take the time to reconnect with her on a deep and cellular level. Know that as you are harming another and harming yourself, so, too, are you harming her. Is this what you want?

Of course not, you say. What, then, must I do to make things right?

Healing the Planet and Ourselves

Now is the time to awaken.

First and foremost, you must make things right with yourself. Everything else will fall into place thereafter.

Your outer (physical) world will change in accordance with the inner (spiritual) changes that you have been able to make.

All pertinent change begins with you. Take the time to embrace this summons, knowing full well that you are up to the challenge.

The only illusion that exists in the minds of men is the belief that all are separate from each other, that all are separate from the Source. Nothing could be farther from the truth (reality). As soon as you eliminate separate consciousness from your life, accepting and working within the oneness consciousness paradigm, you are on your way.

It is time to buckle up for the most adventurous ride of your life, none other than the thinning of the veil. We are honored to be able to assist you on this journey.

Covellite

The Covellite pieces in my life have originally come from Peru. This stone ranges anywhere from a deep indigo blue to black, with a hint of flash (gold, deep red, deep purple) on its surface. Given its color, this is a stone associated with the Brow (Third Eye) chakra (the avenue to intuitive wisdom, also referenced as second sight), another stone that has been ascribed to the developing and/or enhancing of one's intuitive (psychic) powers.

There are several ways in which to utilize the beneficial energies of this stone: you can wear it in pendant form (the one I wear is a majestic wire wrapped pendant, courtesy of Crystalmoon of eBay; referenced in the introduction), you can carry it as a pocket stone (which is something that I like to do), you can meditate with it (my favorite avenue), or you can sleep with it (which is something that I am yet to do).

I was *not* the least bit surprised to discover that Covellite and Nuummite can work very well together.

Healing the Planet and Ourselves

An interesting aside note, Covellite was the first discovered natural superconductor. Superconductivity, as discovered by Heike Kamerlingh Omnes in 1911, refers to an electrical resistance of exactly zero (which occurs in certain materials below a characteristic temperature).

Given that Covellite has no electrical resistance at its own critical temperature level, this means that electrons may travel freely through the material, carrying large amounts of electrical current for long periods of time and without losing energy as heat. In addition, once the transition from the normal state to the superconducting state has occurred, external magnetic fields cannot penetrate it. Referred to as the Meissner effect, such has implications for the creation of high-speed, magnetically levitated trains (Maglev). [8]

Meditating with this stone makes me feel as if I am going on an inner journey; one that may unlock past life memories, in keeping with their importance to the now.

---

[8] Bonsor, Kevin. *How Maglev Trains Work* article. Retrieved August 8, 2010 at http://science.howstuffworks.com/transport/engines-equipment/maglev-train.htm

Healing the Planet and Ourselves

I can almost see a fog creeping in when my eyes are closed, most reminiscent of the originial Twilight Zone shows. A slow and steady beating, like a mother's heartbeat to the newborn babe nestled close to her breast, persists; such a comforting feeling, this is how I feel when working with Covellite.

Slow and steady always wins the race. There is much truth to the fable about the Tortoise and the Hare, is there not? Slow and steady serves to harbor more of an increased concentration, focus and intent, than does a one-shot deal. Truth be told, nothing is ever a one-shot deal, so please do not be misled into thinking that such exists.

You are not here to compete with anyone. There is no competition. All shall be accomplished in its own time, in due course.

There will be an event, a situation, a synchronicity, an aha moment, a virtual signpost, a happening, that will serve to awaken you. When this moment arrives, you shall be ready to embrace the change that is needed.

Healing the Planet and Ourselves

We are very impressed with your recent article, Getting Out Of Our Own Way as posted on your blog, [9] *for this says much that we were wanting to share with you.*

As an author, we feel you are blessed with the ability to write in a fluid, coherent, intricate and literate manner. It is an honour to be able to work with you on this particular written production, for it shall be one most unlike any other.

We know that you like unique; so, too, do we resonate with unique. It can further be said that unique gives one much to contemplate and ponder, which is so very important.

Thank you for taking the time to work with us.

---

[9] Doucette, Michele. (2010). *Getting Out Of Our Own Way* article retrieved on August 20, 2010 at http://www.portalsofspirit.com/blog/

Russian Quartz Record Keeper

From the information that I was given, this very special crystal was discovered near the famous Ural Mountain range in western Russia, an area that is also a vortex (meaning a site of increased energy).

Crystals from vortexes tend to be more powerful. Some feel that the energy from a vortex will heal many health related issues; likewise, they can also assist one in becoming more spiritually attuned. This particular piece is both energetic as well as protective in nature.

A Record Keeper is one that depicts a raised pyramid, or triangle, on one face of the crystal. There are times when you may also see many of these markings on more than one crystal face. In order to be able to clearly see the triangular marking(s), you may need to reflect a light source off each individual face.

Likewise, it is equally important that you carefully check all of the faces of any quartz crystal that comes to you.

The *very first thing* that I look for are these particular triangular markings, some of which can be so minute, so tiny, that it is easy to miss them. One's search must always be a thorough one.

Record Keepers are said to hold information that was placed there, thousands of years ago, from the times of Lemuria and Atlantis. Libraries of stored information, meditating with them will allow you to access their information.

You activate them by rubbing your thumb across the pyramidal triangles.

I am writing this particular entry on Saturday, October 9, 2010, a date representative of what would have been the 70th birthday of revolutionary and visionary genius, John Lennon.

I find much synchronicity between this crystal, one that has come to me from a vortex area, one that clearly demonstrates hundreds of these particular triangular markings, and the individual being discussed.

Healing the Planet and Ourselves

It is quite the exhilarating experience to hold a crystal up to the light in order to examine all of the crystal faces more thoroughly. Experiencing these markings always fills me with a sense of adventure. These are the crystals to which I have an affinity. I trust that I shall continue be worthy of the knowledge contained within their crystalline bodies.

It is believed that the Record Keeper is one of the most sacred crystals because it holds the wisdom and knowledge of the universe.

When a person is properly attuned to a Record Keeper, this knowledge is made readily available. Ancient knowledge that contains profound secrets and esoteric knowledge of the whole of the higher consciousness, it takes both an open mind, as well as a pure heart, to access this knowledge.

That which has been written about us is true. We carry, embedded within our crystalline being, vast amounts of information of a time long since past. Those who work with us must be most patient, as we are not about to give up our secrets to anyone who desires them.

Healing the Planet and Ourselves

There are those today, just as there have been those in the past, who would use this vast knowledge to their own ends; hence, we are most selective in our choice.

We are here to work with those who exhibit a pureness, a genuine caring for the brotherhood of man that shall come to be. Like you, we rejoice in the knowing that the earth shall, once again, become the Garden of Eden.

We, too, were ones to appreciate the words of John Lennon; in particular, those pertaining to Imagine.

As shared by Canadian astrologist Tara Greene, "this song will endure and always keep John's inspirational vision and dreams for peace alive, always reminding and inspiring us to open our minds, to visualize and create a reality of peace, harmony, no religion, no division, no countries, all the people living and sharing life in peace. This is a truly consciousness changing song." [10]

---

[10] Greene, Tara. (2010) *John Lennon 70th Memorial Birthday from True Blue Beatles fan*, accessed on October 9, 2010 from http://infinitynow.wordpress.com/

Healing the Planet and Ourselves

This is a song that "taps into Quantum Physics. If we can IMAGINE it, it begins to be created. John Lennon's singing of the song makes it real. He is the archetypal progenitor of that creation." [11]

While some may say that he was a dreamer, he was not the only one. There are many of you, on the planet today, who are endeavoring to carry out the revolutionary dream that began with the lyrics of Imagine.

This is exactly what must be done to enable the world to be as one, thereby exemplifying the oneness of all creation.

---

[11] Greene, Tara. (2010) *John Lennon 70th Memorial Birthday from True Blue Beatles fan*, accessed on October 9, 2010 from http://infinitynow.wordpress.com/

Blue Celestite

This delightful crystal is a marvelous, albeit sometimes delicate, dusky sky blue color. Almost a celestial color, if you will, its hue is attributed to the presence of minute traces of gold. This is a color that needs to be experienced to be fully appreciated.

Peacefulness and mental clarity seem to go hand in hand for me when working with this crystal. Celestite also seems to calm an over-active mind, to which a great many within the human family can attest. On occasion, I, too, still find myself there.

I also feel a sense of completeness, contentedness and oneness when working with Blue Celestite; a deep sense of relaxation that wants to go on and on and on. As a result, I try to meditate with this stone as often as I can.

In accessing the realm of consciousness, one enters into the realm of quantum physics whereby one must come to understand that consciousness is not the brain.

Healing the Planet and Ourselves

It is most appropriate to say that the cosmos is suffused with consciousness, as is correctly believed by Physicist Freeman Dyson.

Why is it that humans have always assumed the brain to be the producer of consciousness? As it has never before been explained to you, how, then, can one even begin to imagine how consciousness is created?

In accordance with the belief put forth by evolutionary biologists, consciousness just emerges, and, yet, there is no evidence to support such a claim.

Larry Dossey, author of <u>The Science of Premonitions: How Knowing the Future Can Help Us Avoid Danger, Maximize Opportunities and Create a Better Life</u>, *shares that "consciousness can operate beyond the brain, body and the present, as hundreds of experiments and millions of testimonials affirm. Consciousness cannot, therefore, be identical with the brain."* [12]

---

[12] Dossey, Larry. (2010) Fall Issue of SuperConsciousess Magazine entitled The Spiritual Journey accessed on October 12, 2010 at

Healing the Planet and Ourselves

Larry Dossey further proposes that consciousness is neither a thing nor a substance, but, rather, a nonlocal phenomenon.

In keeping, "if something is nonlocal, it is not localized to specific points in space, such as brains or bodies, or to specific points in time, such as the present." [13]

To further make use of his work, nonlocal refers to words such as infinite, immediate, fundamental, omnipresent and eternal; a model that is most cordial to premonitions. Is this not a direct summation of what you are?

Clearly, there is much to be gleaned from the research and understandings of Larry Dossey, MD. [14]

---

http://superconsciousness.com/topics/science/why-consciousness-not-brain
[13] Ibid.
[14] http://www.dosseydossey.com/larry/default.html

Quantum Quattro Silica

Quantum Quattro Silica, better known as QQS, is the trade name that has been given to a combination of five minerals, Shattuckite, Chrysocolla, Dioptase, Smoky Quartz and Malachite, all in conjunction with silicon dioxide (the most abundant mineral located in the earth's crust, with its crystalline form being what we call Quartz crystal). This most colorful stone first appeared about 1996, its location source being Namibia, South Africa. It is important to share here, however, that Gem Silica (Chrysocolla in Quartz) is not the same as QQS.

Interestingly enough, QQS has been touted the Millennium Stone, perhaps because it is said to provide for spiritual maturation, thereby supporting transformation. In minerals that rarely occur together, clearly, there are many gifts to be found within its vibration.

While there are proponents that state it to be immune boosting, I am unable to attest to this claim. I do, however, begin to experience a strong, pulsating energy that rushes throughout the entirety of my body, within mere moments of holding this stone.

Knowing that the energies of QQS are working throughout my physical body, it can certainly be said, therefore, that I feel most energized.

We open with these special words – In La'kech – which is a traditional Mayan greeting, meaning I Am Another Yourself.

It is both essential and important that you take the time to de-stress. How you do this becomes your choice: getting more sleep, talking walks to commune with nature, reading a book that catapults you to a special place, listening to music that revives you, exercising on a more frequent basis, meditating in order to achieve thoughtful silence, treating yourself to a day at the spa.

The ways in which to do so are as boundless as the individual in question. If you do not take the time to unwind, at the end of each day, who knows what can be set in motion with regards to one's physical and mental well-being?

Healing the Planet and Ourselves

All physical dis-ease begins in the ethereal before manifesting in the physical.

If given a chance, acute stress will play complete and utter havoc on your physical body. This is what we are here to help you undo.

Taking the time to investigate the traits and historical significance of each individual mineral that you will find within our crystalline being will provide you with further insight. Please continue reading.

Shattuckite, often found in conjunction with Ajoite, Turquoise, Chrysocolla and Malachite, is a stone with a high copper content, thus making it extremely beneficial for healing.

Chrysocolla is often confused with Turquoise. Having been in existence for thousands of years, in ancient Egypt it was called the wise stone (which is one of the reasons why our dear Cleopatra carried it with her wherever she went).

Healing the Planet and Ourselves

When found within a mixture of Malachite, Turquoise and Azurite, it is referred to as the Eliat Stone (a gem that has long been associated with King Solomon).

The Native peoples say that Chrysocolla strengthens the resistance of the physical body, thereafter filling one with calm.

Dioptase, related to the heart chakra, is a stone that has a dramatic effect on the entire human energy field, thereby serving to balance the entire chakra system.

Malachite, also associated with ancient Egypt, located in the Sinai Peninsula, has a long history, going back as far as 4000 BC. It is a stone that often lined the headdress of the Pharaoh, thereby raising their vibration to a higher frequency level and providing them with the gift of wise council. In truth, the high copper content of this mineral projects a steady pulsing electromagnetic energy field. As a result, Malachite can absorb the negative energies found within the auric field, thereby cleansing the field and balancing the energies of the individual wearing the stone.

Healing the Planet and Ourselves

Smoky Quartz was sometimes known as Smoky Topaz, a most incorrect and misleading term. This is an extremely grounding and stabilizing stone, a stone that brings calm and centeredness to the physical body.

As you can now see, there is much that we are here to assist with.

Life becomes so much more enjoyable when you take the time to de-stress, so we urge you to find that which works for you. Embrace it wholeheartedly.

Maintaining an optimistic and positive outlook will serve you well, for such extends one's physical life. Detract from all things that merely serve to add more negativity because in time, such thoughts, feelings, emotions and reflections will play a part in shutting down the physical body and/or in creating dis-eases that will take over the physical body.

You can do so much more for yourselves. We are here to do what we can to assist you along the way.

aka Boudicca, aka Bliss

Citrine

Citrine was used as a gem in Greece as far back as 300 BC. Natural Citrines are mostly pale yellow in color. It is important to know that most of the commercial Citrine available today, those that are a deep amber color, and sometimes darker, is actually heat treated Amethyst.

The ancient Romans made use of Citrine for beautiful jewelry as well as intaglio work, meaning a cutting style of a stone utilized in order to make a design depressed below the surface of the stone, which, in retrospect, was a form of relief carving (albeit quite different from a cameo design).

Citrine is a stone that balances the Solar Plexus chakra, thereby serving to integrate the lower and higher chakras as well.

Living in the northern hemisphere, we go through extended periods of time, from fall through to spring, without adequate sunshine. Many suffer from SAD, or Seasonal Affective Disorder, myself included.

Healing the Planet and Ourselves

Knowing that this stone carries the healing energies of the sun, thereby increasing one's creativity and energy levels, this has become a very important stone in my personal healing repertoire.

Remember Galileo who published an account of his telescopic observations of the moons of Jupiter, using such to argue in favor of the Copernican heliocentric (sun-centered) theory of the universe and was thusly deemed a heretic and placed under house arrest due to his advanced age, all because he was going against the dominant geocentric (earth-centered) Ptolemaic and Aristotelian theories strongly supported by the Roman (Catholic) Church?

In truth, he was so right in determining the importance of the sun in your world (warmth, light, life), was he not? So, too, are you important to your world.

Many think, feel and believe themselves to be of little value and/or assistance when it comes to raising the vibration of the planet. Many feel inconsequential.

Healing the Planet and Ourselves

By now, you should be familiar with what is referred to as the domino effect.

In bringing sunshine to the life of another, be it through a smile, a kind word, a caring action, they also react and respond accordingly.

This, then, serves to create the necessary ripple in the tapestry of universal consciousness. While you may think your minute action to be of insignificant influence, in effect, the exact opposite is what transpires.

You are so much more important that you realize. You are so very valuable to the overall schemata and yet you believe yourselves to be trivial and nonessential.

You must come to both accept and acknowledge the important role that all have come here to play. In demonstrating a loving, accepting, positive countenance, so, too, do others witness your example, perhaps also experiencing and sharing in it as well.

Healing the Planet and Ourselves

You are more influential than you can ever begin to humanly fathom. Instead of simply seeing puddles, now is the time to begin to focus on their splash.

In applying the Golden Rule to your life, take the time to live your truth, to live your words, to live your knowingness; this is what brings happiness and inner peace.

aka Gemmy

Serpentine

This stone can be many different colors, all due to varied mineral infusions located within the stone itself. In keeping with its name, Serpentine best resembles the skin of a snake.

This stone was prominent in ancient Assyria, a means of asking for double blessings from the gods and goddesses of that time. Stated to be the ideal sculpture medium, Serpentine was one of the most popular stone choices when it came to building cathedrals and museums, as well as widely used objects (such as goblets) in the households of European kingdoms.

It has been stated that Serpentine is the stone to work with when one wishes to activate and raise their Kundalini Energy. This Kundalini activation has long been associated with enlightenment. The experience involves the Kundalini serpent moving up from the base of the spine to the Crown chakra area, a process that can occur spontaneously in some individuals.

Healing the Planet and Ourselves

While it is something that I have never attempted, I can only encourage the individual to read up on all available literature and internet material, before attempting to do so.

Serpentine may also be referred to as New Jade, whereas the Infinity Stone, which is actually a combination of Serpentine and Chrysotile, comes from South Africa.

The very day on which you are writing this dictated entry is a special day of observance for many: Remembrance Day. Mother Gaia is always deeply saddened by any loss of life, and certainly more so when that loss is unexpected and unnecessary, for that, then, upsets the balance of nature.

It is imperative that balance exist.

This means that you must work towards creating balance within your own life. Freeing yourselves from fear so that you are able to trust enough to listen to your hearts, is certainly the place to begin.

How can this be done?

Healing the Planet and Ourselves

Avoid negative influences, people and situations that continue to keep you embroiled. Stop watching TV, stop listening to the radio, stop reading the newspapers as well as reading news related magazines, at least until you have successfully established a place of emotional detachment.

Make use of affirmations to counteract the negative feelings, thoughts and emotions, as they arise.

Pay attention to specific fears so that you can begin to explore, on a deep and introspective level, why they continue to exert an influence in your life.

Take the time to learn from others, while celebrating each success along the way.

Do not be afraid to live simply, detaching, as needed, from the confines of materialism, while also taking the time to integrate your passion (bliss) into your daily lives.

Live in the now, becoming more mindful of every decision and choice that you make.

Exercise on a more regular basis.

Healing the Planet and Ourselves

In short, you must learn to heal this illusion that you refer to as life. Separation does not exist. It has only ever existed in your minds. Until you are able to heal this mirage, you will not be able to actively work towards achieving wholeness.

We know you to be a divine being, a spiritual being, a perfect being. You, yourselves, must also come to this same realization. You need to feel, know and believe this to be truth.

In the words of Mahatma Ghandi ... a man is but the product of his thoughts; what he thinks, he becomes.

To become the peace, love, compassion and forgiveness that you seek, you must think, feel, see, know and believe separation, discord and dissention to be the falsehood. You must emulate that which you desire.

All is created by thought. All is created by intent.

In reshaping your own reality, so, too, do these changes serve to balance the collective consciousness attached to the planet.

Healing the Planet and Ourselves

Taking ownership and assuming responsibility for your thoughts means that you are reclaiming your conscious creative power.

You need naught rely on others for truth. The truth you are seeking resides within.

Always remain true to who you are, creating from the heart. There is nothing more spiritual than that.

aka Dragon

Black Obsidian

As a stone, Obsidian has quite the history, having been used for the making of arrowheads and other sharp tools since Paleolithic times. Black Obsidian, as its name implies, is a pure, glossy black color, produced when felsic lava, extruding from a volcano, cooled rapidly and without any crystal growth. Is it not a wonder, then, that this stone (natural volcanic glass) was used, in ages past, to create ancient mirrors? Black Obsidian was also the favorite stone for scrying (crystal gazing) [15] in order to receive psychic visions and/or impressions.

This is another favorite grounding stone of mine. Author Robert Simmons refers to it as a psychic vacuum cleaner in that it is able to cleanse one's auric field of disharmony, negative attachments and one's own negative emanations (such as anger, fear, greed and resentment).

---

[15] http://www.crystalskulls.com/scrying-crystals.html

Healing the Planet and Ourselves

Black Obsidian, then, can also help keep one's thoughts from turning negative.

The Root chakra is the force that enables, and allows, us to connect with the energies of the Earth, thereby empowering our physical being. This is the chakra that has long been historically connected with dragons and snakes, both of which are symbols for the Kundalini. Black Obsidian is an exceptional grounding stone for the Root chakra.

You are your own scryer. You are your own shaman. You are your own intermediary between the human world and the spirit world; hence, you are able to heal yourselves through spiritual means. Each time you enter a spiritual dimension, you gain the knowledge, power and insight that is needed for such a healing to occur.

Everything you need exists within.

Like the Hermit, you must also take the time, on a daily basis, to engage in thoughtful (introspective) silence.

Healing the Planet and Ourselves

You are here to live lives of unlimited joy, wholeness and well-being. Anything that interferes with this purpose must be re-evaluated. What changes do you need to make so that you can begin to live fully in the now?

Each journey is a personal journey.

All are here to remember, to re-discover, to re-connect with themselves, courtesy of an awakening. Growth takes time, work and contemplation.

You are as the gardner tending to the crop.

What seeds are you sowing?

What are you taking the time to cultivate?

Many are completely unaware as to the nature behind the constructs of both duality and polarity.

Duality refers to physical separateness of opposite, yet related, modes of being: male and female, light and dark, night and day, yin and yang, hot and cold, past and future.

Healing the Planet and Ourselves

Polarity, on the other hand, refers to the essence of the underlying unity of these dualistic pairs, meaning that you cannot have one creative force without the other; that both are needed to maintain creative balance, that both are merely two extremes of the same thing.

Might it be the split between the two hemispheres of the brain that allows one to perceive this duality? Is it, then, a condition unique to the human existence?

What happens when the two hemispheres of the brain become fully integrated? Is this not a most interesting question?

The only person you can change is yourself.

Demonstrate your truth on a daily basis. Live the thoughts of truth that denote who you are and have always been, for in so doing you will show others what is possible to attain.

We salute those of you who have been able to showcase themselves in this manner.

aka Shaman

Shattuckite

Shattuckite was first discovered in 1915 in the copper mines of Bisbee, Arizona (USA); most specifically, the Shattuck Mine. With a predominance of blue shades, there are also other combinations of colors that include turquoise, green, red, brown and cream, indicating other minerals.

All copper rich stones, like Azurite and Malachite, are known to have vivid blue or green colors. Shattuckite, then, is clearly no different.

The high copper content of this stone makes it an incredibly valuable healing tool. It must also be remembered that copper is an energy conductor, meaning that it will amplify energies (including thoughts, feelings and emotions). In addition, the positive influences of copper are said to improve circulation and soothe arthritis and rheumatism. This could well be the intuitive reason behind my being continually drawn to such stones (well in advance of my awareness of their copper content).

Healing the Planet and Ourselves

I feel calm, serene and very grounded when working with this stone.

We, too, are a work in progress, integrating our collective energies in the stone you call Shattuckite. While you are here to focus on your own individual energy, in having done so, such also aids the collective, does it not?

Everything is about ……….

[1] Balancing the energies (meaning thoughts, feelings, emotions, words, responses, actions).

[2] Becoming who you have always been.

[3] Exemplifying peace, love, honesty, truth, compassion, wisdom, wholeness, acceptance ... on a daily basis.

[4] Acknowledging the perfect beings that you are.

[5] Loving, and experiencing, life, in the now, to the fullest.

[6] Eliminating separation, hatred, greed, envy, jealousy and pride from your energies (meaning thoughts, feelings, emotions, words, responses, actions).

Healing the Planet and Ourselves

[7] Living from the heart as opposed to the head.

[8] Taking ownership and responsibility for your energies (meaning thoughts, feelings, emotions, words, responses, actions).

[9] Exonerating the other person because you are solely responsible for you; there is no one to blame.

Life is truly a grand and wonderful adventure that is to be lived.

Do not deny yourself this marvelous opportunity for growth, for change, for self-actualization.

Apophyllite Pyramid

Apophyllites are naturally formed crystal pyramids. This is an absolutely phenomenal crystal for Third Eye chakra activation, making it more receptive to spiritual energies.

Laying down with an Apophyllite Pyramid placed on my Third Eye, I have often received visions and insights (about ongoing situations).

I believe this crystal to be one of the most powerful mineral tools that can be used in reference to allowing one to see the interconnectedness of the universe (which is alive and has consciousness).

All are traversing the path back to God(dess), a path that will ultimately lead to the peak of the mountain, the capstone of the pyramid.

Reflecting back to ancient Egypt and the pyramids at Giza, what was their purpose? Why were they created?

Healing the Planet and Ourselves

Surely you must know that they were more than mere burial tombs. [16]

The builders of the pyramids were masters of sound. Sound is naught but a vibration, a frequency.

Given the dimensions of the internal chambers, it becomes clear that they were well aware of the fact that sound and frequency was a significant part of the creation (meaning manifested thought) equation.

So, too, are we here to assist you in your own metamorphosis. All will embrace this change at different times. This is to be respected and accepted, without judgment.

As you are able to shine your light, you demonstrate what is possible on this plane of reality.

---

[16] Putney, Alexander. (2006). *Pyramid at Resonance* website accessed on November 11, 2010 at
http://www.humanresonance.org/pyramid.html

Dioptase

Discovered in 1797, Dioptase is an uncommon mineral found mostly in desert regions where it forms as a secondary mineral in the oxidized zone of copper sulfide mineral deposits. Its color ranges from intense emerald green to bluish green.

Meditation with this stone is a powerful experience, enabling all to reach their authentic self through forgiveness. Sometime the person you most need to forgive is yourself.

The expanse of life, the duality and polarity associated with life, the vastness and richness of life ... this is what you are here to experience.

While you primarily experience through the noted five senses relative to the human existence, do not forget about the sixth (intuitive) sense, for this consciousness is also a significant part of the overall experience.

Healing the Planet and Ourselves

Life is far more than what can be seen with the human eye, felt with the human hand, tasted and sensed via the mouth, ears and nose.

Life is about knowing.

Life is about believing.

Life is about an ever growing level of awareness.

Life is about recognizing and living your truth.

We are here to be used as a necessary catalyst.

Black Tourmaline

In ancient times, Tourmaline was popular in the Mediterranean region. A likeness of Alexander the Great, dated to around the second or third century BC, carved in India, well confirms the authenticity of this claim. This means, of course, that Tourmaline has been used as a gem for over 2,000 years.

While Tourmaline comes in a variety of different colors (blue, green, brown, red, pink, yellow, green, blue lilac, violet), I am rather partial to Black Tourmaline, also known as Schorl, due to its strong protective properties (which can shield one from harmful electronic equipment emissions).

It appears that Black Tourmaline may also assist your body in reaching homeostasis (the state when your body is working perfectly and all is in balance).

Black Tourmaline is a stone that has long been used by Shamans in African, as well as both Native American and Aboriginal tribes.

Also of Indigenous descent, I am rather partial to its strong grounding effect on my physical body (Root chakra).

Now is the time for introspection and discernment. Now is the time to explore your own soul-self by way of your consciousness.

The logical mind does not always dictate intellectual understanding; hence, you must become more intuitively aware, for this is a great gift. Intuition, when combined with love of self as well as trust, allows for your spiritual awakening.

Always take the time to listen to your heart. While you may continue to use your head, it is of the utmost importance that you learn to rely on what you feel in the depths of your being.

Yours is a life-changing, transformational journey. All, at some point, will traverse this path.

There is much to experience, much to learn and much to integrate along the way.

Healing the Planet and Ourselves

While the road may be fraught with confusion and denial, let not these seemingly negative states distract you from what must be accomplished.

Learning to monitor your thoughts, so that you create only what you desire, will be one of the biggest challenges that you face, but learn this you must. I am here to assist you along the way.

The spiritual reality is such that you are being called to remember who you really are.

You are being called to Become who you really are.

You are being called to embrace and live this spiritual reality.

You are here to achieve a reunion with your soul-self. In wholeheartedly embracing this re-connection while still living within the human, physical form, you will have attained the goal you set for yourself.

Embrace the Now.

Live the Now.

Healing the Planet and Ourselves

Maximize the Now as you go about creating the new earth.

You are present when ... "You state your intentions fully, succinctly and clearly; You feel calm and confident; You allow yourself to feel without apprehension; You act or respond with fear of reprisal; You know when you know and when you do not; You are aware that all options are always available to you; You feel anchored and grounded in your body; Your mind is quiet; Your heart is the source of your expression; Your breath flows easily; You are aware of your conscious existence in this moment." [17]

These are very important words to behold. Take the time to be present.

---

[17] Petrinovich, Toni Elizabeth Sar'h. Sacred Spaces Newsletter, *Be Present or Be Absent*, dated December 25, 2010.

Atlantisite

Atlantisite, a combination of green Serpentine with purple to pink inclusions of Stichtite, is found in abundance near Dundas (Stichtite Hill) on the island of Tasmania. The reader may want to revisit the segment on Serpentine for additional information on that aspect of this particular stone type. In reference to Stichtite, it is formed when continental plates collide. In keeping with a spiritual perspective, it is said that this stone brings higher awareness of one's emotions.

In promoting compassion and forgiveness, bringing a calming and meditative-like peace to one's self as well as one's environment, Atlantisite is a most gentle stone.

It has been noted to activate visionary symbolism from the spiritual realm as well as communication from one's guides (which, in truth, may actually be your Higher Self). This is also a stone that promotes positive thinking.

Healing the Planet and Ourselves

I feel much love and acceptance when working with this stone. While in meditation, I am able to go to my inner still place, that place of quiet, that place of all-knowing; the place where all shall find the answers they seek.

You are God's most wondrous creation, an extraordinary being of much renown, and yet you do not feel worthy. We are deeply saddened by this understanding because you are not yet aware of who and what you really are.

You are here to heal yourselves of much negative baggage (as in separation, fear, doubt, anxiety, worry and frustration, to highlight but a few), for it shall be only then that you can begin to embrace the potential of which we speak.

Forgiveness is an integral segment of this self-healing process.

As Gary Renard, author of both <u>The Disappearance of the Universe</u> *as well as* <u>Your Immortal Reality: How to Break</u>

the Cycle of Birth and Death, shares, "You are Spirit, whole and innocent. All is forgiven and released." [18]

Many of you have such difficulty forgiving yourselves. It becomes in being kind, loving, accepting and forgiving of another that you are also being kind, loving, accepting and forgiving of yourselves.

Every act of forgiveness further undoes the ego, that very part of you that has convinced you that separation exists. In truth, forgiveness is a gift that you are here to give yourselves.

As always, the inner world is a reflection of the outer physical condition. You are here to become that which you seek. As you reflect these particular ideals (peace, love, compassion, unity, acceptance, nonjudgment) on the inside, fully acknowledging them as your reality, so, too, will they be projected outward; in having done so, you become a beacon of light unto others.

---

[18] Renard, Gary. (2006) Your Immortal Reality: How to Break the Cycle of Birth and Death (page 80). Carlsbad, CA: Hay House Inc.

Healing the Planet and Ourselves

Teaching by example is the most effective way to teach others. The spiritual journey is an individual one; as such, it must be experienced singularly.

That is not to say, however, that one cannot learn to practice a healthier, more adaptive way, of relating to that which one sees happening around them; therein lies the importance of teaching by example.

The only way in which to eliminate any negative situation, event or circumstance, is to change the cause. This can only be accomplished through the power of the mind.

In changing the way you see and experience the world, the world around you changes accordingly.

Everything is up to you. In making these integral changes, you must also be patient and kind, loving and forgiving, with yourselves.

Rejecting the programming of the current consensus reality, while not an easy task, is the long-term certainty. This is the role you have come to fulfill.

Healing the Planet and Ourselves

Are you ready to embrace the changes that are needed?

Verdite

Verdite is the trade name for a Fuschite based rock belonging to the Mica group of minerals. A semi-precious stone, Verdite was discovered among some of the world's oldest outcrops of rocks that are 3500 million years old. Also called African Jade, the only known sources are in southern Africa, mainly Zimbabwe, where the best quality deposits have been found.

Based on its age, it has been stated that meditation with Verdite can result in both access and assimilation of ancient knowledge.

It is so very true that life is about living, however, there are so many things that stop you from living; instead, you are merely existing.

Living involves the ability to let go and let God, as your saying goes. Do not allow yourselves to be controlled by the drama of life. You must allow life to unfold naturally. You must learn to enjoy the moment.

Healing the Planet and Ourselves

There is much that you need to do so that you can begin to live life to the fullest.

[1] Changing the way you think, feel and act, both about the world, as well as towards others, is essential.

[2] Accepting the totality of yourself, which includes both light and dark aspects, is an important step towards self healing.

[3] Forgiveness of self is of extreme importance.

[4] Embracing positivity, as the way in which you wish to live and experience life, is paramount. This means that you must learn to release all negativity from your life (as in TV, radio, internet, newspapers and magazines) so that you can learn to detach. This also means that you need to stop watching TV shows that employ violence and negativity, replacing them, instead, with laughter and reassurance.

[5] Exemplifying nonjudgment and compassionate allowing for yourself, as well as others, is also essential.

Healing the Planet and Ourselves

[6] Replacing fear-based programmed beliefs with those that resonate with your own inner truth(s) becomes the prerequisite to inner change.

[7] Reconnecting with Mother Gaia, on a deeply dynamic, vital and intimate level, is what shall bring you back to the simplicity and inherent goodness of day-to-day living.

[8] Knowing, understanding and believing that change is always for the better is the mindset that will allow you to embrace change.

[9] Accepting your divinity, your connection with God, and knowing that you have never been separated from the Creator, is an important step towards Becoming who you really are.

[10] Acknowledging your oneness with God and all Creation, while also living this knowledge, is what shall bring about a heaven on earth atmosphere in your life.

As you begin to live by way of your own example, so, too, will this empower others to Become who they really are.

Healing the Planet and Ourselves

The mind is the power. In truth, as an individual being, you have incredible power.

When you are heart-focused, you are vibrationally balanced.

As soon as you recognize a state of unbalance coming to the fore, take the time to step back, withdrawing your energies. Cease all interactions until you are able to, once again, bring yourself back into balance with the heart.

You must work on creating the life of your choosing. Do not allow yourselves to be swayed or coerced by another. It is imperative that you continue to maintain, and live, your truth(s) at all times.

We wish you much success on this most magnificent journey.

Aka Constance

Purple Jade

It has been stated that Jade was a revered stone with regards to several cultures. Given its smooth even texture, Jade has been a preferred material for carvings, dating back thousands of years.

Jade is as significant in China as Gold and Diamonds have been in the West. It was not only used for the finest objects and cult figures, but also in tombs for important members of the Imperial family. Jade was also associated with the five cardinal virtues: compassion, modesty, courage, justice, and wisdom.

In Central America, the Mayans, Aztecs, and Olmec's also treasured and honored Jade higher than Gold, creating symbolic carvings and masks out of it.

Purple Jade deposits are found in Turkey. Purple Jade (which is of the Jadeite variety) can be found in hues ranging from a light violet to a rich purple, with the lighter colors being more common.

Healing the Planet and Ourselves

Let us get back to the 2012 equation, shall we?

Truly, it matters naught whether the truth as you know it, as you believe it to be, about the Mayans is correct. It is most unfortunate that the mass consciousness of humanity has a tendency to replay the same doom and gloom tactics, over and over and over again, like a broken record, which we believe is a human created phrase, is it not?

Indeed, the planet is changing. You can observe this to be true.

Likewise, humans are also changing. You can observe the transformation and renewal that has been taking place. Many are no longer content with the ego needing to wield its power over another.

Instead, you are needing to realign with heart based consciousness.

It is this realignment of heart with body, mind and spirit that now moves you, for it is time.

Healing the Planet and Ourselves

You need not be frightened by the Galactic alignment of December 21, 2012. Now is the time to embrace this new awakening in yourself.

Please do not allow yourself to become lost in the doom and gloom, death and destruction splash that meets you everywhere you turn.

The time to trust, to believe, to maintain positivity, despite all the negative media hype that exists, is now.

The time to become peace, to become forgiveness, to become love, has long been waiting for you to recognize that it exists.

The time to shed the ego, to live from the heart, to speak from the heart, to transform one's self in service to others, is calling out to you.

Trust in yourself. Believe in yourself. The birth of a new consciousness is now imminent.

aka Maya

Kunzite

Kunzite was first discovered at the Pala Chief Mine near San Diego, California (USA), in 1902. It was named after gemologist George F. Kunz, the first individual to describe it after the turn of the twentieth century. A member of the Spodumene family, Kunzite has also been referenced as Pink Spodumene (the deeper the color, the more valuable the stone).

Mere moments after positioning this stone in my left hand, I begin to experience a distinct tingle in the center of my palm. I feel such peaceful acceptance emanating from this stone, that it enables me to quickly retreat to my quiet place in introspective and meditative silence.

A most energetic stone, Kunzite is a lithium based stone, one which serves to promote calm, while also releasing tension and promoting a more tranquil disposition.

Healing the Planet and Ourselves

As the ego-dominated center is dismantled, all will come to embrace the heart-centered approach to living This is the manner in which all are meant to exist.

A heart-centered approach is one that is very much dictated by intuition and unconditional love. As you come back to embracing this approach, you come back to Becoming who you really are.

Living and loving from the heart gives you the power to negate situations (people, circumstances and events) that can be highly explosive (negative) in nature.

As long as you do not get hooked into providing the conditioned emotional response(s) of the past, you can learn to detach from the occurrence so that you are no longer controlled by it.

Instead, you are able to walk away, letting go of everything that no longer serves you.

As Rasha so accurately shares, "Do not delude yourself into thinking that the world situation is out of control. Quite the contrary; the situation is very much <u>under control</u>. It is *under the moment-to-moment control of the collective mindset, which co-creates it and recreates it in the ever-evolving moment of the now."* [19]

The "adverse conditions with which much of your world is grappling in these times are not the victim-oriented results of random conditions. All of it is energy based. All of it has been created, energetically, by the unified force of the abilities of each and every being here. And every bit of it could be shifted, instantaneously, to conditions reflective of the ideal of All Creation, were the hearts of all focused in that intention. That result <u>can</u> be brought about. That result <u>will</u> be brought about. All that remains are the options of what will be experienced, and by whom, in the process of that shift." [20]

When you feel the need for an instant and deliberate calming influence (from anxieties, worries, depression), know that we are here to assist you.

---

[19] Rasha. (2006) *Oneness* (page 69). Santa Fe, NM: Earthstar Press.
[20] Ibid.

Hiddenite

Hiddenite was first discovered in Alexander County, North Carolina (USA) in 1879. A member of the Spodumene family, Hiddenite has also been referenced as Green Spodumene (the deeper the color, the more valuable the stone). Hiddenite is also strongly pleochroic, meaning that there is a color intensity variation when a specimen is viewed from different directions.

Feeling both a pulsing in the palm of my left hand as well as in the tips of my toes (both feet), I can honestly say that this is a stone that appears to help my entire physical body.

This is a very calming, relaxing stone, one that helps in engendering compassion for others.

Everything you want and dream about is achievable, once you have been able to tap into the power of the mind. However, there is much that needs to be accomplished before you are ready to become a conscious manifesting being.

Healing the Planet and Ourselves

You must first release yourself from consensus thinking (the reality that you have always believed to be true), a process that takes considerable time, but is crucial to the overall equation.

You must also reconfigure your thoughts, words and actions, so that they serve to enhance the positive instead of the negative, otherwise, you merely get more of what you do not want.

These two undertakings are absolutely necessary so that you can advance from creating by default (the unconscious form of creation) to creating with conscious heart-centered intent.

Disciplined thought and disciplined emotion "are skills to be cultivated by all who consider that their focus is in truly being able to make a difference for the overall well-being of the human race." [21]

All will find their way here, when they are ready.

---

[21] Rasha. (1998) *The Calling* (page 50). Santa Fe, NM: Earthstar Press.

Healing the Planet and Ourselves

While every route will be different, given the fact that each journey in an individual one, the end result is always the same: a conscious awakening to the Divine Being that you are, as well as a conscious knowingness that there exists a connectedness with all of creation.

Malachite

The first culture to make extensive use of Malachite was Egypt, going back at least as far as 4000 BC when it was being heavily mined in the Sinai region (near what is now the Suez canal). You could say that copper mining was akin to the first real industry of the ancient world. This stone was prized due to the fact that it was the easiest copper mineral that could be reduced to copper metal.

The ancient Egyptians believed that wearing bands of Malachite, around the head and arms, protected the wearer from outbreaks of cholera that often raged rampant in the area, especially as the individuals who mined the Malachite (more than likely slaves) were often unaffected.

While the ancient Egyptians crafted Malachite into amulets, jewelry and cosmetics (eye shadow), it was the Russian Romanov dynasty who made Malachite synonymous with grandiose opulence.

Healing the Planet and Ourselves

Discovered in the foothills of the Urals, near Ekaterinburg in 1635, the Romanov's were able to easily obtain the Malachite they needed to decorate their lavish palaces. Not surprisingly, this opulence did much to hasten the depletion of this mineral.

Known for its incredible beauty and attractive colors, it ranges anywhere from a rich dark green shade to a lighter green hue. Malachite is a form of copper ore, getting its green color from chromium. Even today, Malachite is one of the most popular semi precious stones available.

Consciousness is the way. It is not enough to learn steadily and to glean knowledge. There is a considerable difference between knowledge and awareness.

Knowledge is akin to the attainment of facts, truths and principles; this, in and of itself, can be most myopic in nature.

Applied awareness is the same as consciousness, which, by comparison, is multifaceted in its nature.

Healing the Planet and Ourselves

Applied awareness (meaning awareness that is lived) is what leads to enlightenment.

This level of understanding "is not born of the process of thought. It is not something that can be taught until the individual is ready to learn. This transcendent state of awareness comes automatically, when one is energetically attuned to shift into a higher gear of one's own consciousness." [22]

In continuation, this "higher level of awareness is no less you than you are. It is not a matter of becoming someone else, for that someone else is you. And as your process evolves, you experience a quickening, wherein a knowingness crystallizes in such an impactful way that it is impressed indelibly upon your consciousness and becomes the only truth possible, at that level of awareness." [23]

Both awareness and the integration of such heightened levels of understanding, then, are the constituent parts of the enlightenment process.

---

[22] Rasha. (2006) *Oneness* (page 101). Santa Fe, NM: Earthstar Press.
[23] Ibid.

Hematite

Hematite's role as a healing stone dates back to ancient Egypt. In addition, there was an ancient treatise written by Azchalias of Babylon (wherein the virtues of this stone were praised) for King Mithridates the Great. [24]

Consisting of iron oxide, Hematite is a very common mineral. In powder form, it is bright red. Ochre is a clay that has been colored by various amounts of Hematite; hence, the red ochre body paint as used by the ancient Picts, the ancient Celts, the Chumash native people of California and the Beothuk of Newfoundland, to name just a few.

Hematite has also been found on the planet Mars, thereby giving the planet its distinctive red color.

I have always felt an affinity with Hematite, appreciating the weight of the stone in my hands.

---

[24] http://www.jjkent.com/articles/history-folklore-hematite.htm

Healing the Planet and Ourselves

Knowing that individuals can be both solid and dependable, so, too, is it with this stone. Hematite is believed to be an incredibly grounding stone.

We are proud to be a grounding factor in this realm. So many feel dazed or spaced out by all that is taking place around them, needing to be solidly grounded in the physical, mental and emotional bodies, if they are to rise above the chaos that appears to permeate your world.

While this chaos is of your own making, there is a way to lessen its effects. We are but one avenue, here to assist you in the beginning stages; all the while, eagerly watching from the sidelines as you eventually come into your own acceptance and understanding of the responsibilities you must reclaim.

Taking back your power is a critical step, a necessary step, towards releasing yourself from the collective in order to concentrate more fully on that which you are, have always been, and will always be.

That which is written in truth, shall always come to pass.

Healing the Planet and Ourselves

That which is written in falsehood, shall always return to its sender (creator), for there is no justice in deliberate disinformation.

A celebratory time, a joyous time, a momentous and wondrous occasion, it shall be when you embrace the fact that you, too, comprise All That Is.

There is no greater alliance to be had, aside from the one from whom you have sprung forth.

aka Affinity

Red Petrified Wood

Petrification is the process by which organic material, such as wood, sea shells and bones, have been turned into stone, meaning that the minerals in the original item have been replaced with a different mineral (usually a silicate compound such as Quartz) while still retaining the structure of the original organic material.

In most cases, the petrification process occurs underground, when wood, or other organic material, becomes buried under sediment and is initially preserved, due to a lack of oxygen.

Generally speaking, the color red, when it comes to petrified wood, means that Hematite, or a form of oxidized iron, was present in the surrounding soil.

Trust, surrender, inner silence and peace are all to be found in the place of one's heart-centeredness. This is the place that you need to retreat to on a daily basis, for this is the place that encompasses the very essence of who you really are.

Healing the Planet and Ourselves

A place of restoration and rejuvenation, this is your home away from home, so to speak.

You are not here to ridicule, torment, judge, gossip or slander.

You are not here to be ruled by fear, guilt, despair, unworthiness or failure.

You are not here to be consumed by feelings of inadequacy, hatred, dissention, unhappiness or denial of self.

You are not here to blindly follow the collective mindset, the governance of laws, rules and dogma, nor are you here to restrict another.

Engaging in any of these behaviors merely results in creating more of the same for yourself.

Instead, you are here

[1] to expand in your knowingness

[2] to meditate within for the answers of which you seek

Healing the Planet and Ourselves

[3] to see that God exists everywhere, within all things and within all beings

[4] to embrace change as the sole constant in your life

[5] to allow all to Be as they are

[6] to Become who you truly are

[7] to experience your own freedom and resolution

[8] to embrace the higher vibration

[9] to move from conflict to harmony

[10] to choose without judgment

[11] to demonstrate compassionate allowing

[12] to be happy, joyful and filled with peace

[13] to be love

[14] to display gratitude and trust

[15] to believe in yourself

Healing the Planet and Ourselves

[16] to be patient and loving with yourself

[17] to learn to become multi-faceted in your truth

[18] to listen to the God(dess) within

[19] to live lives of unlimited joy

As we still retain the structure of our original organic material, so, too, do you still retain the structure of your divine essence.

You, too, must come to that very realization.

aka Petri

Sunstone

Sunstone is a Feldspar crystal that forms in molten lava and is discharged onto the surface with the help of a volcano. As the lava weathers away or is broken, fine crystals are released.

In ancient times, this stone was used by native peoples for barter. The Vikings believed it to be a talisman for navigation. During the Renaissance, Sunstone was associated with the sun, given its sparkling orange-gold hue.

Sunstone from India is particularly popular, with the nicest specimens being a deep orange, coppery sienna, color with a gorgeous inner sheen. It must be denoted, herein, that Goldstone is *not* the same as Sunstone.

Symbolically, Sunstone is linked to Moonstone (another Feldspar crystal). Carrying these two stones allows the energy and influences of the Sun (benevolence, warmth, strength) to harmonize with the energy and influences of the Moon (wisdom, understanding, self-knowledge).

Healing the Planet and Ourselves

It is said that Sunstone lends extra energy at times of stress or ill health. There have also been claims that it can both assist in the contemplative (mind) processes as well as dramatically bolstering one's energy level.

Sunstone is a stone that has always been able to warm my soul and lift my spirits. Living in the northern hemisphere, where little sunshine is experienced throughout the long winter months, many people, myself included, are affected by SAD (Seasonal Affective Disorder). Perhaps I was being intuitively guided all along.

Interestingly enough, as I sit here in this particular contemplative mediation, we are experiencing an intense winter storm, complete with high winds, blowing snow and significantly reduced visibility.

Many have called us liquid sunshine, albeit in mineralized form. If we are able to help anyone suffering from such physical conditions as SAD, depression, anxiety or loneliness, then we are well pleased.

Indeed, our energy is a warm and uplifting one.

Healing the Planet and Ourselves

It is an honor to be affiliated with your Sun, an ancient and wise star. As the Sun kisses the landscape of the planet in its daily sojourn across the sky, so, too, do we seek to provide healing color to the planet.

As most are aware, color can be immensely pleasing, inherently distracting or downright aggravating. Let it be known that you are here to have fun with color.

More than 5000 years ago, the Chinese discovered a subtle energy present in the body; an energy that was not discernible via sight or touch. It was also discovered that "energy disturbances in the subtle bodies precede the manifestation of abnormal patterns of cellular organization and growth." [25]

Many in your time are now saying the same thing: that thoughts and beliefs about health, which often culminate as worries, anxieties and fears, must first exist before they can manifest in the physical.

---

[25] http://tuberose.com/meridians.html

The Chinese "discovered and identified twelve acupuncture meridians along which this energy travels in the human body." [26]

Affiliated with every organ system operating within the body, it can be said, then, that meridians are the distinct pathways of both positive (balanced energy) and negative (blocked energy) life force power.

There are also seven major chakras, or energy centers, located within the human body. Each is linked together through the movement of life force energy as it circulates throughout the physical body.

There are issues that can affect the functioning of both your chakras and meridian systems, thereby leading to a variety of health related problems.

With the blocking of emotions, you are unable to feel. This inability to feel also means that you are not able to release the emotions that are causing the disturbance(s) to the body.

---

[26] http://tuberose.com/meridians.html

Healing the Planet and Ourselves

Allowing yourself to be coerced and controlled by the negative thought forms of others brings about a blockage of your own life force energy and power.

Toxins, be they chemical, metal or atomic, will result in physical health issues unless purged from the physical body. Do take the time to be more discerning about what you are ingesting.

Unbalanced thinking, feeling and behavior will also affect the overall running system. It becomes essential to locate a balance between the physical, mental, emotional and spiritual bodies.

A lack of connectivity to nature (trees, plants, flowing water) can result in the increase of positive ions. With an excess of positive ions, there are many unpleasant physical effects (body pains, headaches, dizziness, nausea, fatigue, respiratory difficulties, allergies, asthma, heart and circulatory disorders) and psychological side effects (emotional unbalance, irritation, exhaustion, apathy, listlessness, anxiety, depression) that can be felt.

In addition, having either an underactive chakra or an overactive chakra can also result in physical disharmony.

What, then, can be done?

First of all, here is something that can never be shared enough.

A healthy diet, combined with clean (vibrant) water and lots of sleep, including relaxation, are key to having healthy energetic systems. As you know, and are continuing to experience on a daily basis, high ongoing stress creates serious damage in both the chakras as well as the physical body.

Smudging your home with white sage will clear away some negative energy blockages.

According to the <u>Ancient Secret of the Fountain of Youth</u> by Peter Kelder, the Five Tibetan Rites exercise program is one that will activate underactive chakras.

Connecting with nature will always have a most profound effect on your energy system.

Healing the Planet and Ourselves

Spending time alone, to internalize the experiences of your day, to meditate, to connect with your Higher Self, to connect with the stillness that exists within, will allow you to maximize living in the now.

Healing with both color and sound; each can also activate the chakras. Crystals and gems, which is where we come in, can also be used to clear blockages in your chakras. Chanting and drumming are most valuable means of maintaining a centeredness, a balance, that is essential; likewise for nature sounds (such as falling rain, waterfalls and waves breaking upon the shore).

Maintaining a passion about something at all times; one that also stimulates the intellect, thereby keeping you engaged (and young) is of extreme importance.

You must take the time to live your bliss.

In this time when changes are accelerating at such a rapid rate, you must take the time to realign yourselves with the All That Is.

Healing the Planet and Ourselves

We are merely here to remind you of these important sources of well-being.

aka Indi

Seraphinite

Seraphinite (or Serefina) is a trade name for a particular form of Clinochlore, a member of the Chlorite group. Mined in a limited area of eastern Siberia, the Lake Baikal region, it is Russian mineralogist Nikolai Koksharov who is often credited with the discovery of this particularly beautiful stone.

This is one of my all-time favorite crystal pieces. With silvery white shimmering patterns, which look like feathery angel wings, on a dark earthy green background, it can be said that the dark green color is representative of the physical (as in Mother Gaia, as in nature) while the silvery white wisps are representative of spirit (as in the ethereal, as in the non-physical). So, too, are we a merger of the physical and the spiritual. As a result, I find this to be a particularly helpful stone for the merging of body, mind and spirit.

It must also be said that Chlorite is an extremely healing stone.

Healing the Planet and Ourselves

I find this stone to be extremely helpful for meditation. This is a stone that, for me, connects both the Heart and the Crown (spiritual) chakra centers, bringing them into further alignment with each other.

Did you know that in fully connecting with your heart (through both increased awareness as well as conscious intent), that you are also connecting with the spiritual essence that is you? It is such a wondrous and momentous occasion when this happens; we eagerly rejoice with you.

Some may refer to this spiritual essence as your Higher Self, and, indeed, there is much truth to this statement. Your Higher Self is, in effect, that part of you which is actually situated in a future reality that resides outside of the linear time that has been imposed upon this majestic planet.

Balance is the key to what is needed by all.

When you find yourself living in balance with the physical, mental, emotional and spiritual elements of you, there exists a deep connectedness and oneness with all life.

Healing the Planet and Ourselves

This is where you find yourself able to begin living a life filled with peace, love and bliss, while also having so much fun in creating that which you wish to express.

You can balance the physical by ensuring that you are getting sleep and exercise. You must also eat well balanced meals. So, too, must you refrain from ingesting foods and drink that serve only to poison the body. Purification of your physical vehicle is crucial.

You can balance the mental by engaging the mind. Take the time to conduct your own research. Do not accept blindly, that which you are fed. You are here to discover your own truth(s), for they shall serve to become your anchor as you weather the storm of change.

You can balance the emotional through detachment and compassionate allowing. In embracing the heart-centered way of living, you must learn to trust yourself, meaning your gut responses and reactions (to situations, circumstances, people and events that unfold). Your experiences shall become your truth(s), so embrace them wholeheartedly.

Healing the Planet and Ourselves

You can balance the spiritual through introspective stillness, knowing that all you need resides within. This is what is referred to as cellular memory.

In a time when balance has become so incredibly important, know as well that this becomes our purpose. We are here to assist you in this manner.

aka Angel

Jet

Jet is a form of fossilized wood (from millions of years ago), similar to coal (or lignite), but harder. The Jet found at Whitby, England, dates to the early Jurassic age (180 million years ago). As a result, Jet jewelry was produced in Britain as far back as 1500 BC. In pre-Columbian times, native peoples used Jet for decorative purposes.

Jet and Amber, then, have a close relationship, both mineralogically as well as energetically (much like Sunstone and Moonstone), in that both comes from trees (with Amber being fossilized tree resin). Interestingly, Jet has also been referred to as Black Amber.

Like Amber, Jet is a neutralizer of negative energies (which also serves to clear one's energy field of vibrations that are not of a harmonic nature).

In addition, both can induce an electric charge when rubbed.

Healing the Planet and Ourselves

In the words of Henry Ford ... thinking is the hardest work there is, which is the probable reason why so few engage in it.

What think you of that statement, we ask? Clearly he meant the type of thinking whereby one was completely and totally engaged in intellectual stimulation, did he not?

The mind, in truth, is all powerful. It becomes in focusing and concentrating the mind that one can attain the levels of thought mastery long associated with the ancient masters. You, too, can become masters of thought.

The power of the mind is where you will uncover all. Feel free to develop this inner mental strength through whatever means (transformational tools) may be open to you, for eventually you will come to both understand and realize (through direct experience) that this is what allows you to become the master that you are.

You will see yourselves becoming influenced, less and less, by the unwanted thought forms that arise in the form of events, circumstances and people.

Healing the Planet and Ourselves

Should a situation come your way, know that you will have the power, the ability, to transform the circumstances, thereby creating something better. Everything pertains to the eye of the beholder, and perceiver, no?

You must find a way in which to remain centered at all times, much like the calm that exists within the eye of the hurricane.

You are here to make the most of the life that you have right now. This is what we refer to as maximizing the now. You can succeed in accomplishing this by remaining positive in all ways, while still holding onto the dream(s) that you wish to achieve.

Mastery of the mind means that you control everything of personal importance: thoughts, feelings, choices, decisions, beliefs, attitudes. Not only is mastery of the mind conceivable, it is achievable.

Mastery of the mind is what leads to the ultimate freedom: peace of mind.

aka Black Amber

Lithium Quartz

This rare stone (a prismatic Quartz crystal with inclusions of lavender or pink lithium) is found only in the remote location of Minas Gerais, Brazil.

A very gentle, but powerful stone, Lithium Quartz brings about an easy state of relaxation (due to the lithium), reducing panic and anxiety attacks, without actually diminishing one's energy level(s). Calming the mind while opening the heart, it is said that this makes Lithium Quartz an excellent meditative stone.

I have been able to witness, firsthand, what anxiety, stress and depression can do to individuals and families. I also know how I feel when personally connecting with Lithium Quartz (the higher the lithium content, the better).

I must also be unequivocal in stating that I am, *in no way*, advocating the replacement of antidepressant medication with lithium based stones. Instead, I am merely commenting on my own reaction to said crystals.

Healing the Planet and Ourselves

R*elax, relax, relax.* It is important that you take time out to engage in whatever it is that serves to relax you. It is essential that you unwind, each day, from the fast-paced, high-stress lives that you lead. Whilst you are engaged in life, can it be said that you are actually living under such driven conditions?

B*reathe, breathe, breathe.* Is not the breath a miracle? Should you not be ever thankful, ever reverent, for this miracle each and every day? Is not the miracle of the breath, the first miracle of truth?

Meditate, meditate, meditate. Take the time to retreat to that special place each day. Embrace the stillness, knowing that you are able to connect with your true essence whilst there.

*****E*****ngage, engage, engage.* Take the time to explore the hidden recesses of your mind. You, and you alone, are responsible for all that you are creating (courtesy of your thoughts, words, actions, choices, decisions, beliefs, attitudes, emotions). There is no one to blame. Take the *time to dissect what it is that you are creating. Are you pleased, or abhorred, with your creation?*

Challenge, challenge, challenge. Is the status quo continuing to work for you? Is the status quo where you want to be? Is the status quo where you want to remain? In your ever-growing control of the situation, be not afraid to think outside the box. Are you ready to break away? Are you ready to take your power back? Are you ready to Become that which you seek?

Accept, accept, accept. You are a spiritual being, a divine being, a creation of the Creator. In truth, you are creators of your own world. Do you like what you see? Do you like what you feel? Can you make it better for yourselves? If so, how? You are here to change yourselves. Whilst you cannot do any more than that, in truth, changing one's self is of monumental significance.

Live, live, live. You are here to rediscover your truth(s). You are here to embrace and live those inherent truth(s), for, in so doing, you become as a beacon unto another, showing them what is possible, courtesy of your own example. Indeed, each soul is but a unique and individual light unto the world.

Love, love, love. This is the greatest truth that exists; the most important truth of all. Fear is simply the absence of love. Eliminate fear, worry, doubt and anxiety from your repertoire, replacing all with love, nonjudgment, compassionate allowing, empathy and equity.

Love is the ultimate freedom.

Take the time to rejoice in the amazing, majestic Beings that you are by Becoming all that you will ever be. This becomes the transformational journey that all must travel. Each and every soul will succeed, for, in fact, you have already succeeded.

We have created a most suitable acronym for you to remember and adhere to.

RBMECALL = Recall **Brain Mastery**

Copper

Copper is an energy conductor, meaning that it amplifies all energy types (including thoughts, feelings and emotions). As a result, pyramids constructed from copper tubing, filled with crystals, make extremely high-energy meditation chambers.

Copper improves circulation, thereby soothing conditions like arthritis and rheumatism. For those who swear by copper bracelets, should they turn green, this is actually a good sign; this means that the bracelets are removing toxins from the body.

In keeping, Copper is the most powerful mineral to use in healing the physical body because it aids in the balancing and strengthening of all bodily systems.

As with any conductor, you must always monitor your thoughts carefully, for thoughts can create in either direction.

Healing the Planet and Ourselves

We prefer to connect with individuals working from a pure intent stance because we, too, prefer our creations manifested under these loving conditions.

You could easily refer to us as your co-creative impetus action.

The time is fast approaching when manifestation shall become instantaneous. This is why it is of the utmost importance to think only of the things you wish to create.

Unbeknownst to a great many, it is just as easy to create more of what you do not want, merely by thinking about them, speaking about them or acting upon them, all from a negative standpoint.

The great masters were well aware of this power.

As you regain control over your own individual life situation, so, too, shall you retain this creative power; a power which exists and is transferred to manifestation by way of conscious intent.

Healing the Planet and Ourselves

It is always in maintaining a continued positive stance, with pure intent, with heart-centered focus, that you will be assisted, when working with us, in expressing and feeling those positive thoughts into manifestation.

A final word of caution, if we may; always remember to be careful about what it is that you are wishing for.

Carnelian

When the tomb of Pu-Abi, Sumerian Queen of Ur (the Mesopotamian capital of pre-biblical times in present day Iraq) from the third millennium BC was opened in 1932, her robe contained Gold, Carnelian and Lapis Lazuli.

The ancient Romans believed Carnelian to be a stone of courage, one that would provide them with strength and confidence.

European history tells us that Carnelian was the gem of choice for intaglios (because its smooth grain surface always separated easily from wax or clay) from the Bronze Age until late Roman times. These seal rings were used by dignitaries and merchants to authenticate documents with their own unique personal signature.

This stone was so revered by the ancient Egyptians that it was one of the three most often used in their jewelry (the other two being Lapis Lazuli and Turquoise).

Healing the Planet and Ourselves

Carnelian amulets called thets (also known as the Isis knot or buckle of Isis, as well as the blood of Isis), were considered sacred to the Egyptian goddess of the dead. Placed on the body of the deceased, Isis was believed to protect the soul (Ka) on its journey through the afterlife. Carnelian was also one of the stones inlaid in the mask of Pharaoh Tutankhamen.

When I need to be energized, much like the Duracell battery, to keep me going and going and going, I simply reach for a piece of Carnelian. Better yet, I put on my 60 inch Carnelian necklace (176 circular 8mm beads) as crafted by Mandy's Gemstones (referenced in the introduction) on eBay. You could then say that I am set for the day; that I am good to go.

Assuredness, this is the emotion that we wish to impart upon you.

Knowing that there exists infinite possibilities, infinite subtleties and infinite realities open to all souls harboring your planet, it is imperative that you remain true to you.

Healing the Planet and Ourselves

How does one accomplish such an enormous feat, you ask?

[1] Take ownership and responsibility for your thoughts, your words and your actions. You alone are responsible for the choices and decisions that are made. You can choose to act in a certain way, or not. Your attitudes are what serve to create your beliefs.

[2] Determine that which is your truth, living this truth as honestly as you can while also further cultivating an awareness in the only constants that exist: love and change. Nothing stays exactly the same. How can it, when you, yourself, do not? All is forever evolving and expanding into something more; embrace change, knowing that as you do, so must your truth(s) change. This, then, is what enables you to Become more multi-faceted in your conscious awareness of life.

[3] Embrace a heart-centered approach to life, for therein exists what can only serve to benefit you on this wondrous journey. While you are here to live out your unique and individual experiences, so, too, are your planetary brothers and sisters. Judge not, lest you, yourself, be judged.

Healing the Planet and Ourselves

[4] Detach from all that no longer serves you whilst on this transformational journey. Your focus must continue to be one of spiritual evolution for your own being.

[5] Existing in the now, take the time to live your bliss each day.

[6] Be grateful for all that presents itself to you, knowing that synchronistic messages shall continue to guide you along the way.

[7] Trust that you shall be able to intuitively discern that which is real.

[8] Know that you are a most noteworthy child of the Prime Creator. In words once spoken to Yeshua, although paraphrased herein, "This is my son in whom I am well pleased;" so, too, are these very words meant for each one of you.

Live well.

Laugh often.

Love much.

Copper Royale

Copper Royale is a stone that is a very solid occurrence of Azurite (blue), Malachite (green), Limonite (green) and Cuprite (red). Extremely rich in copper content, Copper Royale is an effective ally for people who suffer from arthritis and rheumatism. Being an excellent conductor of energy, this stone is a most suitable choice for those who wish to envelop a true spirit of planetary brotherhood.

In having reached the midway point, we are delighted with your continued and sustained efforts. We but wanted to acknowledge and congratulate you, thus far.

As well you know, the time of the Armana Kings, most specifically Akhenaten, was a time whereby an earlier Golden Age was attempted. The people had long been controlled and manipulated by the Priest class. They were told what to think, what to believe, how to worship, how to pray.

Akhenaten attempted to eliminate this control.

Healing the Planet and Ourselves

You are being faced with the very same in your current time.

Controlling influences exist everywhere you turn, be it through the media, subliminal advertising, subliminal programming, religion, education, politics or science.

How can you possibly escape all that constantly assails you?

How can you begin to reassert your own control?

Is it even possible to do so?

You need the assistance of no one "to reclaim your power, to be all that you are, to stand as the creator of your own reality, which, in truth, you are, and to begin to remember this and recognize it and to go within and reawaken that ability. As you do that, those that have sought to control you for so long will find their power dissipating." [27]

This is what you are here to do.

---

[27] Author's note gleaned from the January 1, 2011 BBS Radio Show Recording located online at
http://www.the2012countdown.com/BBSRadio_show_recordings.html

Healing the Planet and Ourselves

Yeshua taught that "the only temple you needed was your physical body, and that all the answers were within you. If you were to go within, you would find those answers." [28]

Akhenaten also attempted to do the same.

Much like the Holographic deck aboard the Starship Voyager, it must be remembered that you are the Prime Creator of your own experience(s) of this particular voyage. Nothing it real unless you give it power.

In thinking about <u>The Velveteen Rabbit</u>, a truly remarkable story, love is the real power, is it not?

As an all-powerful being, to whom have you acquiesced your power?

You must be extremely honest in the answering of this question, for, indeed, you have taken the time to give it away, total carte-blanche as they say.

---

[28] Author's note gleaned from the January 1, 2011 BBS Radio Show Recording located online at http://www.the2012countdown.com/BBSRadio_show_recordings.html

Healing the Planet and Ourselves

Now is the time to reclaim, reaffirm and reinstate this power, creating the very truth(s) and ideals that you wish to live by.

Like the Knights of old, so, too, must you live by your honor. This begins, first and foremost, by honoring your very selves. In so doing, you are also honoring God(dess), for you are they/them and vice versa.

All is One.

All has always been One.

All will always be One.

The time to step up to the plate, to swing the bat and hit that homerun, is now.

The game of life can be one that enslaves you, even to yourself, or releases you to enjoy all that life and living have to offer.

What will your choice be?

aka Egypt

Rutilated Quartz

Quartz, the most common mineral on Earth (found in nearly every geological environment), is a component of almost every rock type, making up about 12% of the earth's crust.

Rutilated Quartz is a variety of Quartz crystal that contains impurities of Titanium Oxide called rutile (which resemble golden needle-like crystal inclusions); a most fetching stone.

Rutilated Quartz existed in plentiful supply for both the ancient Greeks and the ancient Romans. A most attractive and ornamental stone, fancy goblets, as well as other ornamental and religious items, were carved from this stone.

Rutilated Quartz is a macrocrystalline quartz that is prized as a metaphysical stone.

The stillness is relaxing, rejuvenating, illuminating. What you seek can easily be found within, but you must be diligent in taking the time to do so. After all, Rome was not built in a day, now was it?

Healing the Planet and Ourselves

We fail to understand why it is that so many of you do not make this much needed effort to embrace the inner stillness. Yes, adequate sleep can give the physical body what it needs, but you must also work on the mental from within your own center.

It is from here, from this center, from this inner stillness, that you shall also be able to obtain the strength you need to complete the emotional circuit as well.

So, you see, it is like your phrase, as horrid as it sounds, the one whereby you talk about killing two birds with one stone, so to speak. Why, then, would you not endeavor to establish this practice on a daily basis?

The mind is strong.

The mind, in conjunction with the power of the heart, is the strength that all should be working towards.

aka Rutie

Chrysocolla

The gemstone Chrysocolla is often confused with Turquoise. A copper bearing mineral found wherever copper deposits occur, it is also often mixed with Turquoise, Malachite, Azurite, and other copper compounds; hence, the initial confusion.

The name Chrysocolla was first used to describe the stone by Theophrastus, a Greek philosopher and botanist, in 315 BC.

Chrysocolla was derived from the Greek words *chrysos*, meaning gold, and *kola*, meaning glue, referencing the fact that Chrysocolla had been employed, from the earliest times by goldsmiths, as an ingredient for solder, called santerna by the Romans, to weld gold pieces together.

Chrysocolla can act to stimulate the mind while also relaxing the emotions at the same time. In connection with both hemispheres of the brain, Chrysocolla is said to be able to impact both your analytical and intuitive abilities.

Healing the Planet and Ourselves

The energy of Chrysocolla alleviates emotional confusion while expanding your mind to a new awareness with a deeper understanding.

While pure Chrysocolla is much too soft and fragile for making ornamental jewelry, when it is found mixed with Chalcedony Quartz, it can easily be made (cut and polished) into jewelry.

Many of you are now feeling a profound emptiness in that which you do; that is because you are here to create in a new way.

We are not here to judge. It is up to you what you create.

You have the ability to create a better world for yourselves, a world of harmony and balance.

This transformational journey is most profound in its implications. Whilst you are not being reborn in a physical sense, you are being rebirthed from a spiritual standpoint.

Referring back to the message of Yeshua, the only temple needed is your physical body.

Healing the Planet and Ourselves

As you delve within, you will find that which you are seeking, for they are like hidden gems, hidden treasure. This, too, is part of the spiritual rebirth process. Therein, you shall come to know that you have an unlimited amount of creative force energy available to you.

Everything that manifests in this world was created in frequency first. How will you know when, the time is right, to embrace the new frequency of the planet?

It all comes down to listening to your heart; simply listen for the sound of the creative force of the universe; listen and follow. There is no resistance when you are in this flow of the soul.

When energy shifts, it wobbles. Some can see it with their physical eyes; others may feel queasy (which could also translate as dizzy, headachy, feeling pressure in the front of their forehead) without understanding why.

Tuning into these feelings will enable you to understand the energy shifts that are prevalent across the planet.

Healing the Planet and Ourselves

As you are changing and evolving day to day, so, too, is it with Mother Gaia; in truth, nothing stays the same.

It is imperative, however, to maintain a positive mindset as much as possible. Yeshua would often speak of "being in" the world as opposed to "being of" the world.

It is important that you remain authentic to your true self, that you speak only your truth. This, then, is what shall allow you to keep abreast of the happenings of the world, but without being affected by them.

At this stage, you are better able to observe an issue from a conscious standpoint. Instead of imbuing the situation with concentrated energy, you are able to withdraw.

This is the most appropriate action to be taking at this time.

This does not mean that you do not take ownership and responsibility for having been part of the creation of the problem (because, collectively, all are), it simply means that by retreating, if you will, you are assisting in its reduction.

You are no longer attached to the outcome.

Healing the Planet and Ourselves

In making the choice to work with love, everything else (joy, peace, hope, serenity, humility, kindness, benevolence, empathy, generosity, truth, compassion and faith) will follow suit.

You are here to step forward. You are here to learn the beauty and value of conscious creation. In the practice of pure and positive intent, you will find yourselves exposed less to negative situations.

There exists a fine line between judgment and discernment. Judgment involves ego and emotion. Discernment, on the other hand, remains egoless and neutral.

We are not here to judge, nor are you.

There is a shift upon us, one of monumental importance, yes, but it will not bring about the end of the world (meaning its total destruction).

It will, however, bring an end to the world as you have long known it to be, birthing, in its place, a much brighter future for all peoples, a paradisiacal Eden, if you will.

Healing the Planet and Ourselves

The truth is always heard in the heart.

Let your heart become the new foundation stone of your life.

You must also trust that your heart will guide you to do that which you must do for you, remembering, as well, that you shall become the ancestors of the future generations to come.

aka Dama Paquimé

Lepidolite with Pink Rubellite

Lepidolite is a type of mica; a by-product of the mining of lithium. Lepidolite has been used as a source of lithium, which is a multi-functional alkali metal used to create parts for airplanes, lithium batteries (as used for ipods, cell phones, pacemakers, digital cameras, hearing aids, MP3 players, wrist watches) and heat resistant glass and ceramics.

In the course of the 1970's, lithium salts gained popularity as a main ingredient in both tranquilizer and antidepressant medications. Today, lithium medications are still being used to treat [1] depression, [2] agitation, [3] aggression and [4] bi-polar issues, all of which are seen as imbalances in the brain.

With the ability to absorb negative energies, thereby creating beneficial negative ions, Lepidolite is particularly helpful in offices, buildings and homes that exhibit poor air quality. As well, Lepidolite counteracts electromagnetic pollution from TVs, computers and other electronics.

This delicate and gentle crystal eases nightmares, mood swings, fears, anxieties and tensions. It also eases feelings of irritability and hopelessness.

Lepidolite is very soothing and calming. Lepidolite with Rubellite Tourmaline, as is in this particular case, is said to bring happiness, joy and increased vitality, while also inspiring love.

In the course of writing this book, several small computer glitches surfaced and had to be dealt with. I was told to continue to relax, that all was well, that all would be complete in due course. In choosing not to panic, I allowed myself to work with the ebb and flow of the tides as they presented themselves.

Too many of you find yourselves stressed to the max. Likewise, you also find yourselves monetarily maxed to the max. This serves to allow for added tensions, anxieties, worries and depressions to become even more firmly established, which is never a healthy thing.

Healing the Planet and Ourselves

There are many people walking about the planet who have been diagnosed with some form of mental illness, running the gamut from depression and anxiety to bi-polar disorder, as well as schizophrenia; likewise, there are also eating disorders and personality disorders.

Unfortunately, a good percentage of the population continue to react as if mental illness is a highly contagious disease. Identifying only with the disorder, these are the very individuals who are not willing to take the time to get to know the person at the end of the prognosis.

When are you going to sit up and take notice of the fact that, although given a label, people are, first and foremost, people first?

We are not here to take away that which may be needed in the form of prescribed treatment. Instead, we are here to work together with the client, further boosting the overall effects, if you will. Should there come a time when an individual need not continue with drug therapy, as is sometimes the case, we remain here to serve, willingly, in the aforementioned capacity.

Healing the Planet and Ourselves

It matters naught your status. We work with all to alleviate the effects of tension, stress, worry, anxiety, depression and OCD, doing our best to assist each in realigning with their majestic spiritual selves.

aka Sophia

Wild Horse Picture Jasper

Wild Horse Picture Jasper is very rich in color combinations of grays, tans, and dark browns, which create stunning scenic landscape patterns much like that of Owyhee Jaspers and other Picture Jasper varieties, making it the king of Picture Jaspers.

Earthy in appearance, this particular form of Jasper makes me feel more connected, and in harmony, with Mother Gaia. Some might refer to it as a major gemstone of earth consciousness (which may be why the native peoples worked with a variety of Jaspers). As for myself, I feel more grounded and balanced when working with Jasper pieces.

While this lifetime is the culmination of everything that you, as a soul, as a spiritual being, have accomplished, it is your present identity that shall carry you to heights that only you can aspire to, should that be your choice.

Everything comes down to choice. You always have a choice.

Healing the Planet and Ourselves

As you embrace the stillness at the center of your being, you will discover the voice of silent knowingness that resides within.

Having done so, you will, once again, embark on a journey of personal transformation, of personal metamorphosis, much like the butterfly in whom you denote exquisite beauty.

In your world, there exists, what you call, a consensus reality. Consensus simply means that there exists, courtesy of the majority, an opinion of general agreement; hence, your laws, rules and dogma.

The reality of the spiritual world, by comparison, is one that involves the willingness to step away from this consensus reality, into the abyss of the unknown.

That, my friends, is when the real fun begins.

Your focus has shifted. Whilst not fully awakened, you are what we term an awakening individual, meaning that you are now being guided, by that inner knowingness, to seek out other like-minded persons.

Healing the Planet and Ourselves

You will also find yourselves employing considerable discretion in determining with whom you are able to share this newfound information.

The process, towards Becoming who you truly are, has already begun.

aka Wild Horse

Ruby with Kyanite

In the ancient Sanskrit language, Ruby was known as *the king of precious stones*. Ruby, like Sapphire, is of the mineral corundum, one of the most durable minerals, second only to Diamond. It has been shared that this stone encourages one to follow their bliss.

The history of the Ruby dates back to the seventh century BC when first mentioned by Marco Polo. The first wife of King Henry VIII is said to have foretold her impending demise from the darkening of her Ruby.

Kyanite does not retain negative energy, and, therefore, never needs energetic cleansing. It also aligns and balances the chakras.

Blue Kyanite, associated with the Throat chakra, is often mistaken for a good quality Blue Sapphire gem. Black Kyanite is associated with the Root chakra. Both boost and facilitate meditative efforts, while calming the mind and reducing anxiety.

Healing the Planet and Ourselves

An amazing healing combination, it is my understanding that Kyanite helps to keep the energy of the Ruby clear. Likewise, Kyanite also raises the energetic vibration of the Ruby itself.

Are you willing to become all that you are capable of becoming? Are you willing to integrate this knowledge and understanding into physical action? Are you willing to work towards the attainment of the Christ Consciousness that all are here to achieve?

Have you ever come across the knowledge that all human souls leave their physical bodies, during sleep, venturing forth to places where their spiritual selves are refreshed?

Ensuring that you receive adequate sleep each night, therefore, restores both the physical body as well as the spiritual body.

So, too, must you care in other ways for the physical vehicle that you are inhabiting.

Change is all about expanding and evolving.

Healing the Planet and Ourselves

As your spiritual awareness continues to change, so, too, does it expand and evolve. In essence, this is a process that is never ending.

How does one continue to evolve in their knowingness, you ask? They do so by continuing to maximize the moment so as to attain full spiritual expression in the now.

You are not here to change another being, nor are you here to think for that person. In believing this and acting accordingly, however, you will have deprived them of their experience. Would you appreciate this if it were done to you? We think not.

You may, however, share your own experiences with them, thereby encouraging them to trust their own intuitive responses.

As is our experience with you at this time, sharing from a space of pure and honest intent is always a good thing.

aka Ruby

Youngite

Youngite, which is a rare stone to find in the lapidary industry, is a natural breccia comprised of Chalcedony, Jasper and Agate. Likewise, this stone is fairly new to the metaphysical healing market.

This composite gemstone has a Brecciated Jasper center overlaid with a grayish translucent druzy quartz that looks like fuzzy gray velvet and usually fluoresces a pale green (under UV light). The Jasper center ranges in color from a light tan to a very pretty peach or salmon color. Mined in Platte County, Wyoming (USA), it is considered by some to be Wyoming's (unofficial) state rock.

Mira Bai of MoonCave Crystals Creative Designs© shares that "this chalcedony is known for its sparkles of light, similar to the night sky, that can be seen when placed under ultraviolet light. Working with Youngite opens the third eye and facilitates night vision." [29]

Despite resistance from many individuals, it is imperative that you learn to trust your intuitive responses, your inner knowingness, for they are harbingers of a higher truth.

Man created separation for himself when he developed, and began living by, the concept of the ego. You became the creator of your own limitations; never have these been imposed on you by the higher power that exists.

You became isolated as a people, warring amongst yourselves for power and control, all courtesy of the need for safety and survival. In further defining yourselves by way clan affiliation, such led to the subjugation of other nations, other peoples.

The energies of the time were dark and dense. Increased negative emotions led to increased negative occurrences.

---

[29] http://www.mooncavecrystals.com/Properties/Properties.htm#XYZ

Healing the Planet and Ourselves

This is what created the collective reality as it still exists today.

There is a way out of this hell hole, pardon our language, that you have created for yourselves. It is simply this: you must have the courage to break away from the whole in order to act upon your own inner convictions.

In taking responsibility for your own actions, you are also acknowledging that there is no one, external to yourself, to blame. You, alone, are responsible for every choice, albeit limited, that you have made.

Everything is made up of energy, and this includes thoughts, ideas and events. In reclaiming your personal power, in taking ownership for yourself as an individual, so, too, must you begin to consider the implications of every thought and every action, before they are allowed to manifest, because, in essence, you are giving them full permission to do so.

You create with your thoughts.

You create with your words.

Healing the Planet and Ourselves

You create with your emotions.

You create with your daydreams.

You create with your actions.

These are the tools through which you manifest your physical reality.

As you learn to become the detached observer, you are able to step back in order to witness each of these manifesting avenues.

This gives you the power to determine if you can allow them to proceed, unhindered, towards fruition (because they are productive). This also gives you the same power to stop yourself, thereby applying the brakes, while in the act of creating them (because they are unproductive), sparing yourself much unnecessary aggravation.

This is the skill that you are here to cultivate. In addition, this is the very skill that allows one to experience self mastery.

aka Socrates

Amethyst DT Brandberg Channeling Crystal

Brandberg crystals are mined from one mountain area in Namibia, South Africa.

A Channeling Crystal can be recognized by a large seven-sided front face with a perfect triangle on the opposing face. Seven is the number symbolizing the intuition of the Higher Mind and attainment of the mystical truths, while the three symbolizes the ability to express creatively and joyously.

The use of a Channeling Crystal enhances conscious connection with one's accumulated knowledge and wisdom, further facilitating the integration of Body, Mind and Spirit.

They can also be used to access wisdom of experience and enlightenment, which is available on other energy levels and dimensions. These crystals are excellent tools for meditation and conscious work with higher energies of light.

Healing the Planet and Ourselves

Did you know that by consciously shifting your thoughts, doing your utmost to retain them at the most optimum positive level, at all times, that you are actually contributing to the ever increasing positive vibratory level of the planet?

Not only are you feeling, and living, it on a personal level, but, so, too, is the planet benefitting greatly from your conscious action.

It takes time to train yourselves to project positive thoughts; likewise, it takes time to train yourselves to project unconditional love and compassionate allowing.

Stop demanding "that the world live up to your personal expectations. Accept reality as that which is, yet strive to continue envisioning it as it could be; cease pointing a finger at others and placing blame external to yourself. Recognize the part you play, simply by being present, in the Creation of the totality." [30]

---

[30] Rasha. (1998) *The Calling* (page 49). Santa Fe, NM: Earthstar Press.

Healing the Planet and Ourselves

How can you further assist Mother Gaia?

[1] Demonstrate compassion towards all beings and all life forms.

[2] Release yourself from negative situations (be they circumstances, events or people) by walking away, refusing to engage in a battle that exists only because you continue to feed it.

[3] Eliminate the need to want to extract revenge on another; justice is not yours to dispense, at will, like sugar coated candy.

[4] Allow the universe to demonstrate the perfection that already exists.

[5] Teach others about their own inner strength and resolution by way of the example that you can readily provide.

Healer's Gold

Healers Gold is the metaphysical name given to a combination of Pyrite and Magnetite, a stone that is mined in the state of Arizona (USA). Both of these stone types are iron based minerals.

Calmed, grounded and focused is how I feel when working with this particular stone combination.

As difficult and unpleasant as it may be, for friends and family to come to understand the choices that you have made, you must always stand firm in your personal truth(s).

Do not allow yourselves to be thwarted by another. Do not allow your attention to be diverted from the direction that you have chosen to travel. The spiritual path is a path that each must walk alone, for the path of another does not belong to you.

You are here to travel your own path, unhindered.

Healing the Planet and Ourselves

All are both teacher and student; interchangeable roles, really, both, of which, are equally important. Once the lesson has been fully integrated, the student becomes the teacher, thereby facilitating for another.

While the challenge is great, and the trials can be profound, the opportunities afforded you are as limitless as the soul being that you are; another reason that the spiritual path is an individual one.

It takes concentrated effort to maintain one's conscious awareness in the given moment.

It takes concentrated effort to remain heart centered whilst also remaining alert, and emotionally detached, to the happenings around you.

In truth, it is no easy feat, but it is achievable.

Such is the balance that must be maintained.

Such is the balance that you are here to master.

Tibetan DT Quartz

At times, gathered in the Himalayan Mountains, at others, on the Tibetan Plateau (within the geographical boundaries of historic Tibet, which is now part of China), Tibetan Quartz Crystals are noted to hold sacred energy frequencies (that contain a very powerful OM vibration).

These crystals are said to bring knowledge and information concerning healing and spirituality to the user. In addition, they are also said to be excellent enhancers and activators of other crystals.

Tibetan Quartz Double Terminated (DT) crystals can be placed between two chakras to either delete stagnant energy and/or to activate both chakras.

It is believed that DT crystals have the ability to receive and transmit energy from both ends. Double Terminated Crystals have also been used to move sickness from the body by changing negative energy into positive energy.

Healing the Planet and Ourselves

Although some Tibetan crystals are found water clear, this stone is usually grayish clear or cloudy, almost smoky, due the amount of carbon and Hematite in the areas where they are found.

The energies surrounding the planet are affecting all by way of such things as life threatening illnesses, incurable and debilitating diseases, unreasonable actions, heated tempers, depression and helpless despair.

Knowing that each individual is their own healer, detached strength is a major factor to being able to eliminate adverse conditions, such as these and others, that exist within the body, within the heart and within the mind.

It is important that negativity be released from the body; otherwise, this build up could well result in a serious physical condition. In truth, this is a scary time for a great many of you, and rightly so.

You must continue to maintain harmony within your home, your workplace (as much as is possible) and, most importantly, within your heart center.

Healing the Planet and Ourselves

As you are able to sustain this level of balance, you are succeeding in doing your part to mitigate the negative effects within your own immediate surroundings; an action that is more important than many may ever come to realize.

Whilst you cannot expect to manifest a positive outcome if you are controlled by negativity, so, too, must you also make sure that you are not confusing positivity with blind optimism or denial.

Do your utmost to avoid confrontation, using discernment to assess each individual situation. Discord need not exist, if that be your choice.

Acting out of love and compassion for all people, for all creatures, for all living things, will enable you to continue to make the greatest possible contribution in these trying times.

So, too, must you allow others to be in the space that they have chosen for themselves because this is where they are in their stage of spiritual evolvement.

Let your light shine forth through actions taken.

Healing the Planet and Ourselves

Let your light shine forth through attitudes displayed.

Take the time to allow opportunities of growth to present themselves to you.

You are responsible for your own state of BEingness.

Be at peace with yourselves.

Be patient with yourselves.

Know that you are here to love.

This approach, if taken, will be the healthiest transaction that you can perform for yourself, for your families, for Mother Gaia.

Satyaloka Quartz

There is a beautiful and mysterious place in the mountains of southern India, called Satyaloka, a word that means *Abode of Truth*. It is said that the ancient enlightened lineage, preserved at the Satyaloka monastery, dates back to a time when enlightenment was the norm.

There is a tremendous energy vortex at Satyaloka, perhaps the most intense on the planet; a vortex that brings many sages and mystics to the area.

Satyaloka Quartz is the name given to stones gathered around the monastery. Despite their relatively tiny size, Satyaloka Quartz pieces are very powerful (due to the energy vortex).

It has been said, henceforth, that Satyaloka Quartz carries the vibration of spiritual enlightenment, making it a tool for spreading enlightenment throughout the world.

Healing the Planet and Ourselves

Meditation, if practiced properly (which includes grounding and protecting yourselves), can open the doors to your higher mind. As a result, you will be able to access the answers found within your inner knowingness. "Seek and ye shall find" was the message that Yeshua continued to share.

You already have all of the answers you need, but you must learn to listen in contemplative and introspective silence. It is in this profound place that real answers can be found.

Let no one dictate what it is that you will readily experience. You may, however, seek to empower others through the sharing of your own experience(s), so that, they, too, can begin to rise to the fullness of their own potential.

Wisdom is determined by your ability to recognize the truth (when it is encountered). You must trust in your own ability to commune with your Higher Self. This is the very route you must travel in order to begin to reclaim your spiritual identity. When one is on the right path, pieces fall into place with little effort.

It must be remembered that you are an awakening being.

Red Celestial Candle Quartz

The Red Celestial Candle Quartz that resides with me came from Madagascar. These crystals have a bumpy appearance (from hundreds of tiny crystals that coat the sides of the larger crystal) that reminds me of melted or dripping wax from a candle; hence, the name. This crystal has also been called Pineapple Quartz.

Knowing that a candle illuminates and gives light to the darkness, this crystal can be used for intent. Due to the fact that we are the creators of our own realities, it is important to remember that intent is *always* pivotal. In this way, I see Celestial Quartz (also known as Candle Quartz) as being the tool to use in going inward, the tool to use for shining the light within, so that the inner world manifests that which becomes the outer, that which becomes your reality.

It has been written that these reddish brown crystals assist with groundedness (which equates to what I know about chakras).

Healing the Planet and Ourselves

A few days previous to this particular meditation, I had a dream about my deceased mother-in-law who clearly spoke the words *Pineapple Quartz*.

Interestingly enough, I have just validated this particular crystal to be number 66 within this volume.

According to <u>Exploring Numerology: Life By The Numbers</u> by Shirley Blackwell Lawrence, the Master Number 66 refers to creative power, which is an earthly vibration, the "so below where all is manifest in our three-dimensional world" which fits well within the words of this book. She also shares that *woman* is also 66 in its full number. In keeping, it is from the woman that the child is born. [31]

So, too, am I giving birth to this tome.

31
http://books.google.ca/books?id=lKxgglvdbdgC&pg=PA157&lpg=PA157&dq=master+number+77&source=web&ots=GpJtR6NBpF&sig=0qg8kgssKv1bSx_7ceV5DahaL7A&hl=en&sa=X&oi=book_result&resnum=3&ct=result#v=onepage&q=master%20number%2077&f=false

Healing the Planet and Ourselves

When meditating with this piece, the first thing noticed is that I feel a denseness, a weight, that belies its appearance, one that does not appear to exist within the stone itself (unlike, say Hematite and Copper). To me, this seems to imply the underlying strength that this piece possesses.

As the avid gamer is able to attain different levels, one after the other, through continued persistent efforts, so, too, is spiritual evolvement a succession of attainable levels in the same manner; mastery of the game, of course, being the chief aim.

If you are wanting to work with us, long-term, we can assist you in attaining this mastery.

Certainly a most cryptic message, perhaps this, in and of itself, was the answer behind the distinct image and message remaining from my dream.

This has since become the stone that accompanies me on my journey to the stillness within. In that light, we are seeking together.

Faden Quartz

Faden Quartz crystals are usually tabular (flat) in shape and have a thread-like line running through them, one that is always perpendicular to their line of growth.

Found in metamorphic formations, the thread-like line is formed when there is a crack in the main host rock (possibly due to earthquakes or other shifts) that grows slowly, most often creating a tabular (self healed) crystal.

It has been stated that this thread-like line can symbolize the silver cord that connects the soul to the physical self, thereby maintaining the connection to a higher consciousness.

Metaphysically, the stone helps one get the strength and energy to go through personal changes that are necessary and unique to the individual, possibly due to the fact that the growth patterns of these stones was greatly impacted upon through re-growth and self healing.

Healing the Planet and Ourselves

We represent the common thread, if you will, that connects all life to the great and wondrous All That Is; for therein lies the thread of commonality so vast that your human mind, at present, cannot comprehend, and yet it exists as many have claimed.

We are as a telephone connection, a landline, if you will, to that which needs to be explored within.

As a unique soul, you are also part of a monad. The word monad is one that was extensively used by the neo-Platonists to signify the One, meaning the Creator.

Apollonius of Tyana expressed his view of God, the Monad, as being a most beautiful being, one not influenced in the least by prayers or sacrifice. In keeping, this being was also one that cared not about being worshipped. Instead, it was written, by Apollonius, that this being could be reached through direct knowing, a means that discerns absolute truth. Despite his having been born in the first century, such continues to remain true today.

Healing the Planet and Ourselves

Apollonius was talking about one's inner truth, a process that can only be achieved by entering into your own direct living experiences with the now.

You are the essence of pure consciousness; you are absolute truth.

To become a self realized person you must ......

[1] Know and embrace the "real" you.

[2] Detach from the ego.

[3] Take responsibility for past actions, forgiving yourself and others.

[4] Come to the understanding that your relationship with yourself is the foundation of your life (outer world).

[5] Honor each person, for they, too, are on their own unique journey.

[6] See the oneness and interconnectedness of all life.

Healing the Planet and Ourselves

You are all masters; you are the very individuals you have been looking for.

Living in accordance with your own true nature, with what resonates within, is the way that a Master lives, for therein lies your own true direct knowing.

This, too, is what you are here to remember.

Red Rosetta Stone

Red Rosetta Stone is a type of Crazy Lace Agate (one of many varieties of banded Chalcedony, whose curved layers exhibit random curvy and lacy patterns) with a distinctive banding pattern and red color.

Agates occur in nodular masses in rock, such as volcanic lavas, and are one of the oldest minerals on Earth (having been used, it is said, for more than 8000 years).

It ancient Egypt, they crafted sacred scarab beetles out of Carnelian (a type of Agate). In Assyria and Babylon, they made amulets and talismans out of Agate.

A famous collection of three thousand Agate bowls (accumulated by Mithradates, King of Pontus) shows the enthusiasm with which Agate was regarded in the past. Agate bowls were also popular during the Byzantine Empire.

Remember, remember, remember; life in its fullest and purest sense is all about remembrance.

Healing the Planet and Ourselves

To put it as succinctly as we can, you are here to remember who you really are. You are here to fully experience this reconnection in order to assimilate all lived experiences into your Being as soul, as spirit. In short, this is the essence of incarnation upon this planet; a process that is far easier said than done, if we may use your terminology.

Many have chosen intensive experiences as part of the journey before them. One must, therefore, overcome these experiences in a significant enough way (which may actually take more mental work as compared to the physical), otherwise one continues to repeat the same experience(s), over and over again, until all has been understood and internalized.

Life as a human being on planet Earth, while daunting and challenging, is a role in which you are to be commended. In having accepted the challenge, all eventually arrive at the same destination; there is no need for despair.

In relaying to you that all succeed, this means that you are also succeeding in your individual efforts.

Healing the Planet and Ourselves

To remain strong, you must feed the physical, emotional, mental and spiritual bodies by ensuring that you ......

[1] Get enough rest.

[2] Exercise on a daily basis.

[3] Ingest simple, healthy, powerful foods.

[4] Drink ample amounts of water in order to flush your bodily system.

[5] Meditate in a manner that allows you to experience mindfulness.

[6] Spend considerable time in nature, be it through such methods as walking, running, skiing and photography.

[7] Spend considerable time experiencing the rejuvenating effects of water (the falling rain, the pounding surf, resident waterfalls).

Centering and grounding the body in this manner will serve you well when further challenged by unforeseen situations, events, circumstances.

Healing the Planet and Ourselves

It is imperative that you learn to remain firmly anchored in your heart center at all times.

Love is what shall change the way things are.

Embrace that thought.

Live that thought on a daily basis.

When choices, decisions and actions result from pure intent and a heart based focus (meaning love), you will have done much for yourselves and the planet at large.

Therein lies true peace of mind.

aka Remembrance

Dragon's Blood Jasper

Dragon's Blood Jasper comes from Australia. It is a mixture of several minerals which include a deep green colored Chrysocolla, Cuprite (the red) and Fuchsite (which is a chromium mica). The green in the stone represents the Dragon's skin, the red the blood; hence the name of this most dramatic Jasper.

Mica is said to be the second greatest conductor of magnetic energy next to the human brain. Since we are constantly bombarded with excess electrical energy in our modern day environments, extra magnetic energy can help to balance the electromagnetic field of the body.

We agree, wholeheartedly, with the Rasha of which you speak in this text.

Even though it looks as if things are spiraling widely out of control, you can rest assured that they are very much under control (meaning the thoughts, words, actions and mindsets of the greater collective consciousness).

Healing the Planet and Ourselves

If the preceding paragraph does not make you sit up and take notice, we have a problem.

If you are to slay the perniferous foe, if you are to slay the personal dragons that continue to assail you, you must emerge the victor in your thoughts, words and actions, as such is what creates the mindset.

The outer world, as you know, is a direct reflection of your inner BEing. To change the outer circumstance, you must be willing to change the inner mindset.

In sharing the words of Mahatma Ghandi ...... Keep your thoughts positive because your thoughts become your words. Keep your words positive because your words become your behaviors. Keep your behaviors positive because your behaviors become your habits. Keep your habits positive because your habits become your values. Keep your values positive because your values become your destiny.

Not an easy battle, it is one, however, that can be won. Knowing the strength and fortitude that is needed by each individual soul, we are here to assist you in this entreaty.

Healing the Planet and Ourselves

We shall continue to provide gentle, yet persistent, nudges in your direction. As a soul being, you already know what needs to be done. As a physical being, you are here to forge anew this reconnection with Spirit. Therein awaits your destiny of old, your destiny of forever.

aka Mica

Rainforest Jasper

Jasper is an opaque and fine grained form of Chalcedony; it is the containing of organic material and/or mineral oxides that gives it the interesting patterns and colors. A favorite gem in ancient times, as referenced in Greek, Hebrew, Assyrian and Latin literature, Jasper has always been associated with protection. Rainforest Jasper, or Australian Rainforest Jasper, is more specifically known, geologically, as Green Rhyolite.

The green color of this stone reminds me of nature (plants, trees, animals) and Mother Gaia herself. We must also remember that we are not separate from animals, plants or minerals; that all are a significant part of the planetary consciousness.

It is clear that we must treat our fellow human beings, and all other forms of life with respect, for each has its specific role in the greater plan.

Healing the Planet and Ourselves

Feeling as passionate as I do about the Earth, and knowing that it is time to embrace change so that the self may be healed (which shall, in turn, heal the planet), you, too, may find yourself drawn to this stone.

Rainforest Jasper is said to be able to balance the yin yang (masculine and feminine) energies; an absolutely critical aspect to self-healing.

If you but take the time to look at the colors exhibited within the lush rainforests of South America, you will see that these pieces exhibit the most magnificent of colors. This is one of the reasons why I am particularly drawn to this stone.

Mother Gaia lives within the colors that project themselves from within our mineral being. As each soul being is unique, so, too, is each individual mineral specimen unique unto itself.

Part of the overall plan, there is a specific stone (type, color, formation) for each being that is drawn to the mineral kingdom.

We are honored to work with our human family in this way.

Healing the Planet and Ourselves

If it is grounding you want, you have come to the right place. If reconnecting with Mother Gaia is what you need, so, too, have you come to the right place.

There is much to explore. There is much that awaits you beyond the horizon, but it ultimately becomes your choice to either move forward, unhindered, into the land of the unknown, the unforeseen and/or to retreat, broken and defeated, in your unwillingness to embrace change.

Neither will be judged by anyone other than yourself, but do try not to be overly harsh with yourselves.

You derive strength from every experience faced, every experienced loved, every experience explored; at some point, this becomes the very strength that will allow you to move forward.

All are here to succeed in this amazing endeavor.

We are but here to serve you along the way.

Clear Quartz Cathedral

While Cathedral Quartz may appear to be composed of several separate pieces (creating that parallel stepped or layered effect, whereby the formation is said to resemble cathedral organ pipes or spires), all are part of the main crystal (which has multiple terminations with at least one point at the apex).

Cathedral Quartz, the same as Cathedral Lightbrary Quartz, is touted as being the light worker and wisdom bearer extraordinaire of the crystal kingdom, more than likely because Cathedral Quartz is akin to a cosmic computer that contains the wisdom of the ages.

It is believed that Cathedral Quartz makes itself known every two thousand years to aid in the evolution of consciousness by raising thought to a higher vibration.

I have also come across the term Atlantis Temple Quartz as being the same as that of Cathedral Quartz.

Healing the Planet and Ourselves

Many of your kind thrive on riddles, others less so. While we do not particularly care for such subterfuge, we are well aware of its importance. Many have come to your world, in years previous to this, many who had no choice but to speak in parables for those with ears to hear.

The time is fast approaching when such tactics shall no longer be necessary, for such knowledge will be readily available to all who quest for truth.

In reflecting on the massive Gothic structures that were created by the Knights Templar, there is still much to be gleaned. With their advanced intelligence of alchemy, both metallurgical and spiritual, they created places of majestic beauty.

Aligned purposely with ley lines, these structures were employed to utilize energies from Mother Gaia in order to energize the human body. It has also been stated, and rightly so, that these Gothic Cathedrals were created as the very energy centers, courtesy of sacred geometry, that were needed to assist in perfecting the human form.

Healing the Planet and Ourselves

By perfection of the human form, we simply mean the healing of humanity to the point whereby spiritual knowledge and spiritual mastery is once again used to benefit and glorify humanity in its creation.

The labyrinth located within the Chartres Cathedral, built around 1215, is also one of supreme magnificence, its purpose representing the inner path that man must travel in order to reconnect with the source that exists within; an experience that ultimately serves to calm the mind while also bringing peace and comfort.

The balancing of both hemispheres of the brain, through many differing means, further allows one to remain on the spiritual path, uninterrupted; meaning that wholeness of body, mind and spirit is attainable.

It is important to denote that all will travel this same path.

There is so much more to human history than both meets the eye and has been written. This, too, shall come to the fore. All will glean an increased understanding of where you have been and where you are going.

Healing the Planet and Ourselves

As the great female Celtic warrior, Boudicca, has been reputed as saying ... gwir achos 'r byd ... Truth for the world.

Truth is what always sets you free.

Embrace your truth.

Live your truth as honestly and as fully as you are able.

This is our message to you.

Amazonite

Amazonite is actually a green variety of microcline Feldspar. While Feldspars are the most abundant mineral to be found within the earth's crust, the green variety is a rare occurrence (possibly due to trace impurities of lead and water). When light is reflected within the crystal structure of this mineral, we get what is referred to as the schiller effect; one that is similar to iridescence.

Ornamental objects carved from Amazonite have been found in ancient Egypt. Part of the Egyptian Book of the Dead was engraved on Amazonite. In addition, jewelry crafted from this stone was found in the tomb of Pharaoh Tutankhamen.

Success starts on the inside, not the outside.

As far as your health is concerned, all parts of yourself (the physical, mental, emotional and spiritual) need to be attended to, or balanced, in order to cure any health problem that may arise.

Healing the Planet and Ourselves

So, too, is success holistic in the same way.

It is hard to think in a successful manner when you are surrounded by negativity; hence, the reframing of your thinking has become an essential piece of the success puzzle.

Likewise, you must also limit, and/or eliminate, the amount of time you spend with people who are negative.

You always have a choice.

You do not have to listen to anything that you deem negative. Neither do you have to internalize such. Instead, you need to control where you place your attention, your energy, your focus.

In keeping with the Greek myths featuring Amazon women, recognized for their great skill in battle, so, too, are you capable of annihilating the enemy called negativity.

It would please us greatly if you were to avail of our assistive energies in this campaign.

Blue Lace Agate

Blue Lace Agate was discovered on Ysterputs Farm in Namibia, South Africa, by a man named George Swanson. Having come across the stone on his farm, a stone of swirling blues and whites that appeared to resemble soft clouds in a blue sky, he coined the term *Gem of Ecology* for this stone.

While Agates are plentiful, Blue Lace Agate is not.

Stillness of mind is crucial.

Stillness of mind is achievable.

We are here to help, primarily in this regard. Meditating with us will allow you to experience the feeling of calm, serene, assuredness that is needed at this time.

Gaining release from the chattering mind is far from being an easy task.

We are here to acknowledge your efforts.

Healing the Planet and Ourselves

As you continue to work with us, you will come to understand the importance of learning to become the detached observer to your thoughts, your feelings, your reactions.

This is the key step in achieving peace of mind, remembering also that peace of mind leads one further toward stillness of mind. Do you see how it is all interconnected?

A most arduous and grueling task, taking continued effort over an extensive period of time, it is, however, a most revealing and rewarding one.

Do not the more Herculean aspects of life become the most relieving, unburdensome and gratifying when surpassed?

If you are willing to stick with the program, if we may use your words, we can help facilitate the changes that are needed.

Rainbow Fluorite

Fluorite (formerly called Fluorspar) has long been regarded as one of the most colorful semi-precious stones in the world, primary colors being purple, blue, green, yellow, followed by rarer pink, red, brown and black. Fluorite can also be found in multiple colors with color zoning or banding being displayed, as is the case with Rainbow Fluorite.

Incredibly beautiful healing stones, I have found Fluorite to be particularly beneficial for the mind. When I am heavily involved in my genealogical researching, this is a stone that assists me with the organization of information. Likewise, it also serves to link this newly obtained information with what has already been known to me. When I am heavily involved in research for the purpose of study, Fluorite is a stone that seems to improve my concentration so that I can see things more sharply, more clearly.

As you can see, Fluorite has become an important stone in my current collection.

Healing the Planet and Ourselves

As Yoda shares with Luke in Star Wars ... "Do or do not do; there is no try." Is this not a paradox of sorts?

Might this be because trying to do something does not have the same energy signature as simply doing it? Could this also be the reason for failure when many of you simply try to do something?

The conscious waking mind is heavily influenced by the demands of family, friends and society, as well as the pressures to conform to dogma, rules and laws. The conscious waking mind is also heavily influenced by the ego.

In wanting to create desired experiences for yourself, as compared to unwanted experiences, you must be prepared to completely bypass the conscious mind in order to access the subconscious mind.

In learning to focus your mind on an aspect that you feel you need to change, you become increasingly aware of the fact that you are able to create your own reality, through subconscious mind activity, attracting to yourself that which you are focusing on through the power of intent.

Healing the Planet and Ourselves

In short, this is what is meant by The Law of Attraction.

In your perpetual quest for knowledge, you seek a place whereby you can turn inward for peace; you seek a place whereby you can access the answers to the deepest questions of life.

In paying attention to your life as it unfolds, in the here and now, you are experiencing Zen.

In experiencing a mindful, nonjudgmental, presence, so, too, are you experiencing Zen.

In becoming the detached observer (without responding) to your beliefs, ideas and opinions, you are also experiencing Zen.

Likewise, in acting as one (by becoming more spontaneous and more intuitive) with yourselves, with others, with the world, you are experiencing Zen.

Zen has often been likened to experiencing a state of Being and not-Being.

Healing the Planet and Ourselves

By direct association, it is the dedicated practice of Zazen that can often lead to Zen.

Zen cannot be described; it can only be experienced.

Zen is both the realization as well as the expression of your truest nature.

That having been said, Zen is the purest state of mind that you can attain; hence, Zen can lead to enlightenment.

Aqua Aura Spirit Quartz

Aqua Aura Quartz is Clear Quartz that has been exposed to pure vaporized gold (which amplifies the conductivity of the quartz itself), resulting in a rich blue color (with subtle flashes of iridescent rainbow color) called Aqua Aura. This alchemical crystal is a fusion of nature and science.

Given the resultant color, Aqua Aura crystals can assist with the Thymus (thymic) chakra, located between the heart and throat under the sternum (collar bone) and slightly to the left where EFT Practitioners direct their clients to locate the sore spot that they continually reference.

The Thymus (thymic) chakra, also referred to as the 8th chakra, is the link between the emotions of the heart and the reason(s) for the intent behind the words that you speak.

We have trouble speaking when we are upset because the flow of energy from the heart is always meant to be peaceful and loving, which is the kind of vibrational energy that this chakra relates to.

Healing the Planet and Ourselves

It has been shared that an open and balanced Thymus (thymic) chakra results in being open to higher spiritual levels (unconditional love, selfless love, connecting your dreams, wishes and aspirations with waking reality). By comparison, an overactive Thymus (thymic) chakra results in being so open to higher spiritual levels that you lose the grounding that it necessary to maintain a connectedness with the physical. In continuation, an unbalanced Thymus (thymic) chakra might refer to one who often indulges in religious and/or spiritual platitudes while ignoring the needs of others. Lastly, a blocked or closed Thymus (thymic) chakra indicates that the individual rejects, and is fearful of, the higher spiritual realities that exist. They may also be unable to express their heartfelt emotions. [32]

Spirit Quartz is a most unusual variety of quartz. The main body of the crystal is covered with small termination points. In some circles, they are referred to as Cactus Quartz or Porcupine Quartz, both terms being most apt descriptors.

---

[32] *The Thymic Chakra (High Heart Chakra)* website accessed on January 14, 2011 at http://www.kheper.net/topics/chakras/Thymic.htm

Healing the Planet and Ourselves

Do you remember the story of Midas, whereby everything he touched turned to gold? While this is not to be taken literally, so, too, do you have this same ability.

Gold, in this case, can be taken to represent the perfected state of being; a state of being that assists the Higher Self to manifest through one's physical form. Whilst this potential has always existed, we are here to help you direct it into being.

Likewise, we are here to assist you in the balancing and healing of your chakras (and, as a result, your auric field). When all is balanced, when all negativity has been released, there is a more flowing, peaceful energy that can exist within and without the body. So, too, does this aid in the inner healing that is deemed paramount at this time.

When meditating with us, we serve to bring forth peace of mind.

When you exhibit peace of mind, you have been granted the much needed freedom from fear, from anxiety, from worry, from stress, from unnecessary tension.

Healing the Planet and Ourselves

When encapsulated in fear, you cannot exist as the loving being that you are.

Allow us to assist you in this necessary release.

Moldavite

This was the very first crystal that made me feel completely comfortable within my human body. Long had I been feeling disconnected from Mother Gaia and my place within the overall scheme of things.

Given the meteorite shower, in the Moldau Valley of Czechoslovakia, between 15 and 20 million years ago, surrounding material was fused together by heat and pressure produced by the impact. This material was then physically catapulted back into the atmosphere. It is further believed that friction with the atmosphere is what resulted in Moldavite, the only gem to have come to us from space.

It is believed that Moldavite was the green stone associated with the Holy Grail; as such, it has been treasured for thousands of years.

In the Middle Ages, Moldavite was reserved only for individuals of royal and/or noble birth.

Healing the Planet and Ourselves

Due to its powerful metaphysical energy, Moldavite is what continues to help me release what is no longer needed for personal and spiritual growth (old ideas and beliefs as well as outdated mental and emotional habits that no longer serve).

Having always needed help with integrating myself into this physical existence, Moldavite continues to assist me in finding comfort, within this physical body.

In the past, we have been referenced as being the Stone of the Grail as well as the Stone of Shambhala, for indeed we are a stone of tremendous power.

In having attained the Holy Grail, you will have manifested your Higher Self into your current physical form. This is the change that you, yourselves, have long been waiting for. Can the same not be equated with Shambala?

In their workings with us, many have experienced the clearing of blockages and the opening of the meridians, all of which has lead to further physical, emotional and spiritual healing.

Healing the Planet and Ourselves

So, too, have many experienced an increase in what you refer to as synchronicity.

Others have experienced more vivid and meaningful dreams.

In continuation, many have also experienced deeper and more powerful meditations.

It must be clearly stated that these notations are also reflective of the shift in your own energies (when working with us).

It is the awakened and fully realized BEing that becomes the Holy Grail.

Herkimer Diamond

Herkimer Diamonds are beautiful double-terminated quartz crystals which are found mainly in Herkimer County, New York (USA). Incredibly, these phenomenal gemstones are found in Dolomite rock that has been dated close to five hundred million years old.

The majority of the Herkimer Diamonds have eighteen faces with six triangular faces forming the termination points on each end of the crystal, which are further separated by a group of six square or rectangular faces. It is this particular hexagonal conglomeration that often results in a diamond shape.

Herkimer Diamonds were formally discovered in the late 1700's.

Herkimer Diamonds often display the sparkling clarity akin to Diamonds; hence the name. Amazing amplifiers of energy, Herkimer Diamonds are said to assist with balance on all levels (mental, emotional, physical).

Healing the Planet and Ourselves

In the process of the spiritualization of matter, you are steadily working towards achieving enlightenment while still remaining within the confines of the physical body. We are here to applaud you in this commanding regard.

Radiating a harmonious energy, we are able to assist in the purifying and cleansing of the body, be it the physical, the emotional or the mental. You can, therefore, expect to feel an increase in your energy levels when you are working regularly with us.

If you are drawn to Moldavite (the Starseed stone of choice), a piece that acts as a catalyst for spiritual transformation and evolution, then we three (you, us, the Moldavite) can work together in amazing ways whereby you are allowing us to encourage more conscious awareness (on your part) of this specific growth process.

Please remember that we are also able to magnify (strengthen and amplify) the energy (frequency) of other stones, depending on that which you are looking for and/or are drawn toward.

Clear Quartz

Quartz is the second most abundant mineral found in the Earth's continental crust (after Feldspar).

While there are different varieties of quartz, Clear Quartz (also known as Rock Crystal) is often referred to as the Master Crystal in that it absorbs, stores, releases and regulates energy, meaning that it can [1] draw off negative energy of all kinds, thereby creating negative ions (which, in turn, creates positive vibes while also clearing the air of stagnant and stale energy) [2] neutralize background radiation, including electromagnetic smog or petrochemical emanations, [3] balance and revitalize the physical, mental, emotional and spiritual planes, and [4] cleanse and enhance the organs and subtle bodies.

Negative ions are believed to produce biochemical reactions that increase levels of the mood chemical serotonin, helping to alleviate those afflicted with depression, mood disorders, chronic fatigue or Seasonal Affected Disorder (SAD). In addition, they relieve stress and boost our daytime energy.

Healing the Planet and Ourselves

You may have experienced "the power of negative ions when you last set foot on the beach or walked beneath a waterfall. While part of the euphoria is simply being around these wondrous settings and away from the normal pressures of home and work, the air circulating in the mountains and the beach is said to contain tens of thousands of negative ions – much more than the average home or office building, which contain dozens or hundreds, and many register a flat zero." [33]

Positioning various crystal clusters in different rooms of your home can assist with the creation of these much needed negative ions.

Given that it contains the whole spectrum of colors and can be used for many different purposes, Clear Quartz also amplifies the properties of other stones.

Does this not sound like a Master Crystal to you?

---

[33] *Negative Ions Create Positive Vibes* article accessed on January 14, 2011 and posted on the WebMD website located at http://www.webmd.com/balance/features/negative-ions-create-positive-vibes

Healing the Planet and Ourselves

While we cannot compete, in either color brilliance or iridescent sheen, with many of our mineral brethren, we are, indeed, the Master Crystal as many continue to attest.

Like the Herkimer Diamond, so, too, are we able to magnify (strengthen and amplify) the energy (frequency) of other stones.

While we can be programmed, it was such an act that brought about the destruction of Atlantis. We now prefer to work with you as opposed to being programmed by you. There is a major difference between the two.

Your working with us will result in increased clarity of thought and purpose. We are also here to help you establish a strong connection to your Higher Self, if that be your wish.

Some have even referred to us as a type of etheric radio. You might say that we have a considerable connection or two.

While you could refer to us as being an emotionally neutral stone type, we will amplify any emotion. Be careful, therefore, what it is that you are broadcasting.

Healing the Planet and Ourselves

As to our packaging, we come in a wide range of crystal formations, namely; Barnacle, Bridge, Candle, Cathedral, Chandelier, Channeling, Crystal Cluster, Double Terminated (DT), Dow (Trans-Channeling), Elestial, Faden, Generator (Merlin), Growth Interference, Herkimer Diamond, Isis, Japanese Law Twin Crystal, Key, Laser Wand, Left Activation (time link to the past), Lemurian Seed, Lineated, Manifestation, Phantom and Included Quartz, Rainbow, Record Keeper, Rutile Inclusion, Right Activation (time link to the future Scepter Quartz, Self Healed, Singing Crystals Tabular (Tabby), Tantric Twin, Transmitter and Window ... so feel free to explore with any, and/or all, of us.

We are here to be enjoyed by you in as much as we are here to work together in achieving your destiny.

You are the very ancient souls that you have been waiting for.

We, too, have long been waiting for you.

Eudialyte

Found at several locations around the world, Eudialyte is still considered to be a reasonably rare stone. Most of what is currently available comes from Russia's Kola Peninsula. While it can be found in a variety of colors, it is the rich magenta colors that are always the most popular.

Eudialyte contains cerium (a malleable metallic rare earth element). It often contains yttrium (a metallic element occurring in nearly all rare earth minerals) as well.

If Eudialyte is held for just for one hour, it has been written that a measurable increase in both Alpha and Beta brainwave activity will have taken place. Beta waves are related to the conscious mind. Alpha waves are associated with the dreaming mind, creative states and ESP (especially clairaudient capabilities).

While I cannot attest to this shared information, I can certainly say that Eudialyte is one of my personal power stones.

Healing the Planet and Ourselves

As a heart based stone, we are here to remind you that as long as you live from your heart, you are expressing the divine energy that resides within.

While there is no one path to follow, all paths eventually return to the one Source. You are allowed to choose the path that feels right for you. So, too, are you allowed to create a life of your own making, of your own manifesting.

We can assist you in making these personal choices of great import.

In honoring the self, so, too, are you honoring the All.

In loving the self, so, too, are you loving the All.

In respecting the self, so, too, are you respecting the All.

In cherishing the self, so, too, are you cherishing the All.

In accepting all aspects of the self, so, too, are you accepting all aspects of the All.

As you gain in universal awareness, you quickly come to the realization that the divinity of another is yours as well.

Healing the Planet and Ourselves

When you respond to people with love and compassion, you readily move from conflict to harmony. Such is the very freedom sought by all.

When you remember, embrace and share your divinity, you free others to walk their truth. You become accepting of their truth, for such is whom they are.

You are here to remember that all are continually evolving and changing as per their own individual experience(s), for this is what adds to both the greater collective experience as well as the totality of God.

In essence, this means that God is also continually evolving and changing through you.

God allows you to express as you choose, without judgment.

You alone determine how, and to what degree, you are to progress along your evolutionary path, moving past your illusions of limitation to the freedom that lies beyond.

You are here to create the life opportunities of your choice.

Healing the Planet and Ourselves

The ultimate question that all must answer becomes: what is it that you choose to create for yourselves?

Scepter Quartz Crystal

It has been written that Scepter Quartz crystals were used in Atlantian and Lemurian healing ceremonies. A symbol of power, those who carried a Scepter Crystal were in a position of authority as high priest or high priestess.

Given its name, this crystal actually looks like a ruler's scepter; there is a rod at the base with a crown-like configuration on the top. Not surprisingly, therefore, Scepter Quartz is an excellent configuration for transmission of directional energy.

We are a specialty crystal formation with much power; most definitely not for the faint of heart. We are here to empower you to employ, on a daily basis, that which you hold true.

What is the point in your talking the talk, to use your terminology, if you are not willing to walk the talk, so to speak? While there are many, among you, who talk the talk, there are even fewer who walk the talk.

Healing the Planet and Ourselves

Be bold. Be brave. Embrace your truth while living it to the fullest, each and every day. This is what is meant by the walking the talk idiom.

There have been individuals brave enough to walk the talk, speaking their truth aloud, challenging the status quo, who have been obliterated. Do not let this deter you from your path of spiritual transformation and evolution.

Be not afraid to embrace who you are Becoming, who you have always been, who you will always be.

The time is now for you to come into your own, as they say.

In surrendering to the divinity within, in surrendering to the will (desire) of the heart, you are able to revert back to your truest nature: a being of love and compassion; therein lies the power belonging to each and every one of you.

It becomes the acknowledgment of this, your truest nature, that further cements (establishes) this power.

Prehnite

Prehnite was first discovered in South Africa by Hendrik Von Prehn. Von Prehn was a Dutch colonial army officer, a baron and a mineralogist. So, too, was he Governor of the Cape of Good Hope Colony. Finding the specimen there, he brought it to Holland in 1774. Von Prehn died in 1785. The mineral he introduced to the world acquired his name in 1788, after his death, making it the first mineral specimen to be named after a person.

A rarity until the early 1980's, finds in Australia have made it more readily available (and, therefore, less precious).

The Prehnite pieces that I am familiar with have either been a very soft light green or a yellow/green, each with a high gloss translucency.

The Prehnite cabochon that I am meditating with comes from Australia.

Healing the Planet and Ourselves

It is your will (ego) that appears to be the driving force of humanity. As long as you are governed by your ego, you are unable to transform on a spiritual level.

However, the moment your will (desire) becomes enmeshed with your heart, a true forging of mind and soul, with the heart residing at the helm, rest assured that the body will follow suit.

This marks the beginning of spiritual metamorphosis.

In speaking words from the heart, in accessing answers from the heart, in remaining guided by the heart as you go about your day to day mindful living activities (with the conscious mind, formerly known as the ego, remaining in the background), you will have returned to your truest nature.

You will have become the Empress, the creator.

With the Magician, the ideas are made real.

With the High Priestess, the ideas attain form.

The Empress, however, is the Mother who gives birth to the creation made real.

Healing the Planet and Ourselves

It is imperative that you continue to remain firm in this BEingness of love and compassion, showing others, by example, what is possible.

It is equally essential that you continue to create your reality (meaning both inner and outer worlds) in this manner, for therein lies the very freedom and peace of mind that all seek to achieve.

Variscite

Variscite is a relatively rare phosphate mineral. The colors vary from light hues of green with bluish tints to darker shades of green, which is why it is sometimes confused with Chrysocolla or the greener forms of Turquoise. It is usually veined with other minerals which make for the most wonderful web-like patterns.

I have found Variscite to be a most soothing stone that helps calm the mind. The cabochon that I am meditating with comes from Australia.

Many are searching for meaning in their lives. In some cases, this has involved past life regressionist work.

We fully understand and acknowledge your need to embrace the past, to explore the past.

We know that, in doing so, you are making an effort to try and discern the now, for there is much that, as of yet, you can neither explain nor fully understand.

Healing the Planet and Ourselves

We do, however, caution you. One can get so caught up in trying to assemble the puzzle pieces of the past that they forget all about being here to live, to explore, the now.

All that you know is the now.

All that you have is the now.

All that exists is the now.

Whilst today will always become yesterday, it is imperative that you take the time to live for today.

Like the hard drive on a computer that stores all pertinent computer files, so, too, can your subconscious mind be compared to such an analogy.

The subconscious mind is home to everything that is not located in the conscious mind, such as previous life experiences and memories; your original files, so to speak.

In order to gain access to this databank of information, in order to make changes to the original files, you must bypass the conscious mind.

Healing the Planet and Ourselves

This is what allows you to neutralize the negatives of the past (because memories cannot be changed) in order to gain the positives in the now.

Acceptance and forgiveness of the past is crucial if you are to move forward.

This may well be the most important aspect associated with past life regressionism.

The most important person you are here to forgive and heal is yourself. From there, things can only get better.

Rhodonite

Rhodonite gets its name from the Greek word *rhodon*, meaning rosy. Its rich pink color is often contrasted with black dendritic inclusions of manganese oxide.

A strong and durable crystal, Rhodonite has been a popular carving material for the last few hundred years, especially in Russia. Whole slabs have been used to carve the sarcophaguses for Czars and Emperors. During the Easter celebration, Russian children would exchange eggs carved from Rhodonite.

In times of antiquity, Rhodonite was given to travelers as a protective stone because it was said to warn them of imminent danger (by way of the heartbeat having accelerated suddenly).

The cabochon that I am meditating with, a super bubble gum pink color with fine detail, comes from British Columbia, Canada.

Healing the Planet and Ourselves

For those of you who believe in a heart-centered approach to life, we are here to reiterate that nothing is more important than living and expressing from the heart.

In truth, we are here to promote love in the form of enabling you to deduce that which is your spiritual passion, your life mission, your bliss, for all are one and the same.

This form of love also involves using your talents to bring love and happiness to others; a direct sharing from the heart.

It is also true that talents can be used to effect positive change.

As you contribute to the world in this manner (living your passion whilst sharing these gifts with others), know that you shall also receive in kind by way of situations that present themselves in the most synchronistic of ways.

Lazulite

A rare semi-precious gemstone, Lazulite is often confused with Lazurite, Lapis Lazuli and Azurite. First described in 1795 from deposits in Austria, its name comes from an Arabic word *lazu*, meaning heaven.

According to an old legend, Lazulite was born out of a giant upheaval of the universe when pieces of sky and sunlight were captured and held by Mother Earth. [34]

Given its intensely deep azure blue color, Lazulite is a stone that has been designated as a psychic (Third Eye) and intuitive stone.

The Afghanistan cabochon piece that came to me was cut from Lazulite within a marble like matrix or base rock, with very finely formed crystals in the matrix stone.

---

[34] http://www.minerals-n-more.com/Lazulite_Info.html

Healing the Planet and Ourselves

In working to pursue greater focus and self-discipline when it comes to mental pursuits (be it study, research, meditation and/or the development of latent psychic abilities), know that we are here.

Exercising the mind, wherein you are thinking freely and clearly for yourself, is paramount. So, too, is rediscovering the power of the mind.

The mind, as most can attest, works in mysterious ways; so much so, that you do not fully comprehend the workings of your own mind.

Your mind is also a very powerful tool. If used correctly, the mind can shape and change your current reality, enabling you to reach higher levels of self-awareness and consciousness.

The unconscious (hidden conscious) mind controls at least 90% of your thoughts, meaning that it is the subconscious mind that represents your mind power.

Healing the Planet and Ourselves

The biggest hurdle towards learning how to create from a deliberate and conscious perspective, this power is not to be underestimated.

Until at least part of this latent consciousness has been mastered, nothing really begins to happen.

Allow us to assist you in making things happen.

Sugilite

One of the newer gemstones to come onto the market in recent years is Sugilite, having only been discovered in 1944 by the Japanese geologist Ken ichi Sugi. It is slowly becoming extremely popular, most notably for its deep purple color. Sugilite is also known under the trade names of Royal Lavulite and Royal Azel.

It is paramount that heart and mind learn to work in conjunction (unison) with each other.

It is a well known fact that those who live and follow their passion feel a sense of wholeness and life abundance, for they are living their bliss (as per the Joseph Campbell of your time). This is what we refer to as spiritual living.

Outside of spiritual living, you are merely going through the motions.

If you are satisfied (contented) with your life as is (meaning maintaining the status quo), we are not the stone for you.

Healing the Planet and Ourselves

If you wish to make fundamental changes in your life, we are here to accommodate.

Moonstone

Moonstone belongs to the large mineral family of Feldspars. It is an opalescent stone which can range from colorless to blue, peach, green, pink, yellow, brown or gray with a silvery sheen. In addition, the clarity of the stone can range from transparent to translucent.

With a sheen that is similar to moonlight, these stones began to be referred to as Moonstone. Also identified as being adularescent, this means that both the hue and the saturation of the color changes when it is moved around.

The Romans believed that this stone was formed by the light of the moon, wearing it as jewelry in 100 AD. An extremely sacred stone in India, Moonstone is deemed to bring good fortune, tender passion and prophetic abilities.

The energy of Moonstone is balancing, introspective, reflective and, of course, lunar.

Healing the Planet and Ourselves

A stone of mystery, long have we been a dreamy and intuitive stone affiliated with the Goddess (the Great Mother, the feminine). Spending time with us will allow you to observe the hidden truths that reside within the depths of your inner being.

Seek and ye shall find.

Take the time to know thyself.

Meditate with us, if it be your wish to embark on a journey deep into the self.

Just as there are tides and rhythms pertaining to the cycles of the moon, so, too, are there cycles in your life. It is imperative that you make note of the wisdom and self-knowledge that increases with each additional journey around the sun (which is our way of indicating yet another birthday each year).

Life is to be lived. Life is to be experienced. Life is to be explored.

Take the time to rejoice in this understanding.

Phenacite

Phenacite has often been mistaken for Clear Quartz or Clear White Topaz. While it is one of the most brilliant white gems known, it lacks the play of color possessed by the Diamond. Ranging from clear to milky white, they often resemble pieces of broken glass; hence, this is a stone that often gets overlooked.

It has been stated that Phenacite has one of the highest crystal vibrations, yet discovered, that connects one's personal consciousness to one's spiritual consciousness (linking the Crown chakra to the Third Eye chakra), further enabling spiritual awareness. As a result, Phenacite increases one's personal vibration.

In the same way that Clear Quartz enhances the effects of other crystals, so, too, does Phenacite work well with other stones.

If metamorphosis of a spiritual nature beckons to you, we can assist greatly in this regard.

Healing the Planet and Ourselves

Thinking outside the box is a terrifying prospect because it equates to acknowledging that change in one's life, which can be a fearful process, is needed. Having recognized that change is paramount, the process begins.

[1] Accepting the premise that you are 100% responsible for the changes that you wish to impart upon your being, knowing that you can no longer defer your thinking to someone outside of yourself.

[2] Understanding that thoughts, words and actions are energy based.

[3] Becoming aware of your thoughts, your beliefs, your actions.

[4] Removal of negative influences (previously programmed beliefs, people, places and situations).

[5] Harnessing the power of the subconscious mind in order to make desired changes to the conscious mind (which includes living from a positive mindset).

[6] Developing and cultivating a positive mindset.

[7] Maintaining a positive mindset through whatever means are deemed necessary (which may well include books, CD programs, metaphysical tools and spiritual teachers in the beginning).

[8] Learning to become a detached observer by becoming a witness to your own mind.

[9] Learning to transcend the dualistic mind by stilling the chatter of the mind (through such means as meditation or brainwave entrainment).

[10] Demonstrating mindfulness on a daily basis.

[11] Embracing your passion.

[12] Living a heart-based approach to life.

[13] Demonstrating nonjudgment.

[14] Demonstrating compassionate allowing.

In short, in order to change your world, as many of our brethren have already attested, you must begin by changing yourself.

Healing the Planet and Ourselves

We quite understand the prospect of such a transformation to be deemed a terrifying change, for it is a fear of the unknown that persists, but change you must if you are to become a self-realized individual.

This is a key component to why you have come, to why you are present on the planet at this time.

In making such an inner and profound change, so, too, are you assisting Mother Gaia in her personal alteration as well. In helping each other, the complete change becomes less dramatic and more gradual.

Thinking of our time together as a marvelous adventure of the soul, we are here to guide you every step of the way.

Chiastolite

Chiastolite is a variety of Andalusite. It is also known as the Cross Stone because of the natural cross-like pattern that is formed when carbon rich impurities form an axis along the crystal.

Discovered in Andalusia, Spain, it has long been used as a talisman or amulet (since ancient times) for protection in warding off the evil eye. It also came to be known as the fairy cross because it was believed to aid contact with magickal beings and entities.

We offer protection from adversarial foes such as [1] the egoic mind, [2] negative thoughts, [3] negative words, [4] negative actions, and [5] unconscious spontaneous reactions to a situation.

We are here to present you with an increased sense of your Authentic Self through such terms as [1] eternal, [2] divine, [3] limitless, [4] powerful, [5] transcendent, [6] infinite, [7] unbounded and [8] complete.

Healing the Planet and Ourselves

You are the creator of your own reality. To change the outer (behaviors, responses, outlook on life) you must change the inner.

In the words of Leonardo da Vinci ... One can have no smaller or greater mastery than mastery of oneself.

As energy, you have always been connected to Source.

We are here to assist you in re-connecting with Source.

We are also here to help facilitate the feelings of strength, power and fortitude at having re-established this connection.

To thine own Self you must be true.

Long have we been waiting for this day.

Super Seven

Super Seven, also known as Melody's Stone or Sacred Seven, is a combination of seven powerful minerals; namely, Clear Quartz, Rutile Quartz, Smoky Quartz, Amethyst, Lepidochrosite, Goethite and Cacoxenite.

Discovered in the region of Minas Gerais, Brazil, an area also known as *Espirito de Santo* (Holy Spirit), makes this a tremendously potent offering to these current times. This stone often displays what appear to be tiny flames of fire. Some have even likened the colorful display in the stone to the Aurora Borealis (Northern Lights).

I see this stone as linking all of humanity; one that may well be able to change the vibratory level of the planet itself.

Each mineral specimen is unique to its own combination (of minerals); such is the same with each of you.

Does this not make life more fascinating, more intriguing, more engaging?

Healing the Planet and Ourselves

Take the time to embrace that which contributes to your sense of wholeness (study, research, reading, writing, genealogical pursuits, exercise, meditation, dancing, singing, acting, music, painting, photography, pottery, drawing, sketching, working with crystals, travel, book clubs, social networking) and well-being.

There is nothing to be said for the hustle and bustle, fast paced, stress filled lives you have created for yourselves. The biggest thing that you can accomplish, and that which can lead to overall healing, is to embrace the stillness of the mind through whatever means you have available to you.

You must learn to still the chatter of the mind, for that, in turn, will also lessen the needless chatter of the physical body.

There exists no need to be in competition with another. In giving the wholeness of yourself back to you, so, too, are you gifting Source.

Nebula Stone

Nebula Stone was discovered in a remote mountain region in Mexico (1995) by Ron and Karen Nurnberg. This dark green, nearly black stone, is covered in green nebula like formations which actually resemble eyes. It has been written that it is like "looking into the birth of a universe in each stone, reminding us of where we came and where we all return" [35] meaning to stardust.

This stone is not to be confused with Kambaba Jasper. [36]

Does not the word nebula make you think of the majestic universe, a universe of unknown possibilities?

How does it make you feel to know that your NASA scientists are now discovering new planets, all courtesy of the Kepler space telescope that was launched in March 2009?

---

[35] http://soul2soultreasures.com/nebula.htm

[36] http://www.nebulastone.com/Kambaba_Jasper_is_NOT_Nebula_Stone.htm

Healing the Planet and Ourselves

One could certainly refer to this as a golden age for astronomers, could they not?

In truth, you are not alone; you have never been alone, despite this long instilled disempowering belief. Representing the vastness of creation, it is our intention that you also come to know, understand and experience this great expanse of which you are a meaningful and noteworthy part.

There is much that continues to remain unknown to you. Do not allow the unexplained, the unexplored, the unforeseen, to hinder your growth in any way. If you embrace these changes in confidence, cognizant of that fact that you can trust your inner self, your heart-based consciousness, know that you shall be guided (by your intuitive self) every step of the way.

Learning to trust, in complete confidence, is a process that heals.

Chrysoprase

Chrysoprase is considered the most valuable stone in the Chalcedony group. Frederick the Great, of Prussia, highly favored this beautiful, opalescent, apple green stone, adorning his palace at Potsdam with objects and furniture made from Chrysoprase. So enthusiastic was Frederick's patronage of Chrysoprase, that for some years his interest alone notably increased the prestige (and price) of the stone.

This stone was also the favorite of Queen Anne, of England, remaining popular all the way through the reign of Queen Victoria

Although Chrysoprase has been mentioned as early in history as 23 AD, it was not mined commercially until about 1740. This stone was also popular in the time of the Greeks and Romans, whereby it was cut into cameos and intaglios. In Egypt, it was set next to Lapis Lazuli and also made into beads.

Healing the Planet and Ourselves

During the time of Alexander the Great (356-323 BC), some began calling Chrysoprase the victory stone.

A being of compassion, you are here to re-learn how to live from the heart, how to remain in your still center, at all times.

In so doing, you must release the ego by uniting your personal will with the inner urgings of the heart. This marriage, a necessary one for the ascension process, will then serve to create a unified force of significant energetic vibration. Such a feat requires much emotional strength.

Likewise, there is courage that must be found within when facing a difficult and/or threatening situation. In addition, you must also learn to remain firm in your resolve.

As a unified force connected with the Great Mother, as well as one of the rarest and most valuable of the Chalcedonies, we can relay her strong healing energy to those who elect to work with us. We consider this to be our mission.

aka Gaia

Tangerine Quartz

Tangerine Quartz comes from Minas Gerais, Brazil. Due to the inclusions of iron (resulting from Hematite) in the cavity where they grew, this is what creates their natural orange color. Whenever I am feeling sluggish and depleted of energy, this is a stone that works well for me. Tangerine Quartz is also a suitable stone to use when working on the Sacral chakra (governed by creativity, intuition and balance).

Meditating with us can lead to new and inspiring ideas. So, too, can we assist you in the expression, and implementation, of those objectives.

Should a writer experience what you refer to as writer's block, as you have at times, we encourage them to work with us. It is in this capacity that we work with the Sacral chakra.

Many find our color to be energizing, vibrant and invigorating. If we are able to uplift someone as a result, then we are well pleased.

Moss Agate

This is a stone that assists me in maintaining a connection with Mother Gaia, given the moss-like pattern inclusions within the stone, a feature that makes it look incredibly earthy.

Many refer to Moss Agate as a talisman in that it is said to bring about abundance in crops for farmers as well as beautiful, healthy flowers for the gardener.

This stone also allows me to experience a sense of freedom and space within my own little corner of the world.

Not really an Agate in the truest sense, we are actually a member of the Chalcedony family. With dendritic inclusions of moss colored green minerals, we represent the energies of the Great Mother.

We can support those who are in need of connecting with the energy of the Earth in order to feel a physical groundedness in the body.

Healing the Planet and Ourselves

It is this very groundedness that further enhances feelings of balance and stability.

Knowing how essential this is, we make ourselves readily available to you.

If we are able to leave you with an important message, it is this: all things are provided for within creation.

Amethyst

Amethyst is a variety of Quartz that ranges in color from pale lavender to a deep, rich purple. The color purple has long been considered the traditional color of royalty; hence, Amethyst has been used to adorn the rich and powerful monarchs and rulers. With fine Amethysts featured in the British Crown Jewels, this stone was also a favorite of Catherine the Great.

Pliny wrote that Amethyst was named for its color, being nearly the same as that of wine. Early Greeks believed that drinking wine from an Amethyst cup would prevent intoxication. Leonardo da Vinci wrote that Amethyst was able to dissipate evil thoughts and quicken the intelligence.

Believing that Amethyst was thought to encourage celibacy and symbolize piety, this stone was very important in the ornamentation of churches in the Middle Ages (church books, altars, pectoral crosses and panagias). Considered to be the stone of Bishops, many wear Amethyst rings today.

Healing the Planet and Ourselves

In Exodus 28:15-20, Amethyst is referred to as one of the 12 precious stones worn by the high priest Aaron in the Breastplate of Judgment.

The royal purple color of Amethyst has also been used to symbolize Jesus.

In Tibet, Amethyst is considered to be sacred to Buddha.

If you are drawn to meditation, whether it be as a method of stress relief or one dedicated to spiritual transformation, you will find us to be an excellent aid. With continued use, we are able to assist in stilling the mind.

When the mind is silent, happiness reigns inside and out. More mentally and physically relaxed, you are then able to move into the higher states of consciousness.

All of this serves to create an enhanced state of balance and well-being.

What you are thinking and feeling (or vibrating) right now has a definite and direct impact on your immediate future.

Healing the Planet and Ourselves

That having been said, you are not your thoughts and you are not your feelings, despite the fact that they are an integral part of the physical experience.

Transcending the dualistic mind is the battle of surrendering the bullying of the mind (ego dominated existence) to mindfulness (an awareness of your thoughts, words and actions).

Mindfulness means being aware of the moment in which you are living.

Mindfulness is meditation in action, allowing life to unfold without the limitation of prejudgment.

Mindfulness means being open to an awareness whilst becoming an Infinite Possibilitarian, a term coined by Norman Vincent Peale.

Mindfulness pertains to existing in a relaxed state of attentiveness, one that involves both the inner world of thoughts and feelings, as well as the outer world of actions and perceptions.

Healing the Planet and Ourselves

To stop acting, instinctively, on the prompt of each and every thought ... this is the gateway to enlightenment.

To cleanse the mind completely, to make it silent ... this is the gateway to enlightenment.

To become a completely conscious being ... this is the gateway to enlightenment.

While we are not here to be dominating or domineering in any way, ours is a strong energy. Some are able to work with us, others not. We urge you to feel free to experiment.

Selenite Rose

Selenite Rose, also known as Desert Rose, is a mixture of the minerals gypsum and barite in rosette formation, hence the rose connotation. These natural sculptures form in arid, sandy environments through the evaporation of shallow salt water basins. While gypsum roses usually have more clearly defined (sharper) edges than barite roses, their crystalline structure is less hard.

With a name that comes from the ancient Moon Goddess Selene, there is very little history on Selenite as a power stone. Too soft to be considered a good gemstone, it is believed that this mineral configuration can enhance clarity, improve self awareness and fortify one's purpose.

We, too, connect with the energy of the Great Mother. Our formations are most unique. Those who are drawn to roses are often drawn to discover what lays hidden beneath our petals of gypsum and sand.

Healing the Planet and Ourselves

Did you know that the oldest rose fossil, dating back more than 35 million years ago, was located in the state of Colorado?

Petals represent layers; layers that must often become exposed in order to reach the epicenter of one's existence.

We are present to offer encouragement with this particular metamorphosis.

Do not be put off by this necessary process of inner growth.

Angelite

Angelite, or Blue Anhydrite, was discovered in Peru in 1987 (during the Harmonic Convergence), the result of the de-watering of the mineral gypsum. The most popular colors are both the light blue-grey and the lilac-blue varieties.

If immersed in water, Angelite will convert back into gypsum, so do not wear this stone while bathing or swimming.

Angelite brings inner peace, tranquility, calm and focus to its meditator.

Life and living is not about stress; that was never the original intent. Living is about experiencing the fullness, the completeness, of life. Even joy can be expressed amidst sorrow.

The purpose of life is to be part of it. The key is to live life consciously. Likewise, you are here to live fully and with intent.

Healing the Planet and Ourselves

As you continue to expand in both your knowingness and your wisdom, so do you continue to expand the consciousness of all life, which is what God is.

To be happy, to be joyful, to be filled with peace: this is the way back to the kingdom within.

To know that God is not separate from you, to know that you and God are one and the same: this is the way back to the kingdom within.

You are here to live lives of unlimited love. You are here to live lives of unlimited joy.

If you choose to have these conditions in your lives, then you must first become that which you want to experience more fully.

If you are seeking serenity, tranquility and inner peace, we are pleased to be here to be able to infuse you with these soothing energies.

Blue Apatite

While Apatite comes in a variety of colors (colorless, yellow, blue, green, brown and gray), my favorite is the vibrant, gorgeous, dark aqua blue colored stone. Although Apatite is a common mineral, gem-quality Apatite is quite rare; as is the case with many stone types, the more intense the color, the more valuable the stone.

As a meditation or awareness tool, Blue Apatite is said to help you maintain focus, concentrate effectively, think clearly, and communicate better.

There is nothing worse than stagnant energy.

You feel as if there is no place to go, no place to turn.

Your get up and go, to use your words, has up and left.

We are here to stimulate your mind into action. In working with us, you will discover that our energies are anything but stagnant.

Healing the Planet and Ourselves

Often times you are in need of a creative solution to what has long appeared to be an insurmountable problem.

Once a solution has presented itself, you are immediately filled with a more uplifting energy.

This is our chief purpose at this time.

Visualizing a life, for all, whereby there are creative solutions to be found for every so-called unsolvable problem is the gateway to recreating a Brotherhood of Man, as denoted by John Lennon.

We are only too eager to be able to support you in this particular visualization.

Aquamarine

Aquamarine is a blue or turquoise variety of Beryl (the same family that Emerald, Heliodor (Golden Beryl), Goshenite (colorless Beryl), Morganite (Pink Beryl) and Red Beryl also belong to.

The Greeks were the first to document the use of the Aquamarine gemstone (around the time period 480 to 300 BC). Legend tells us that Aquamarine amulets were worn by ancient sailors to ensure safe and prosperous passage across stormy seas.

Writers of the Middle Ages claimed that Aquamarine, when cut as a crystal ball, was thought to be a superior stone for fortune telling.

Aquamarine is mentioned in <u>Gemmarum et Lapidum Historia</u>, an ancient and important gemological work compiled by Anselmus De Boodt, published in 1609.

You are a melding of God-man (the mind of God expressing in human form) and man-God (physical man expressing the

Healing the Planet and Ourselves

God within), a combined merger of spiritual and physical that serves to continue the expansion of God(dess) into forever.

In this light, you need not seek anything outside of your Being, for all that you need resides within.

As you come into your own alignment with truth, you, too, shall denote that anything that does not serve you, anything that is not in resonance, shall fall away.

Willing to embrace the higher vibration, an internal shift in consciousness takes place, thereby enabling you to Become (who you truly are).

Become who and what you truly are by listening to the God within you.

Become who and what you truly are by both knowing and accepting that God speaks through feelings, for they will be your guide to truth, directing you onward toward your individual path of enlightenment.

Healing the Planet and Ourselves

You are here to embrace, communicate and live that which is your highest truth. Ultimately, this is the end result of the spiritual evolution process.

This is the very mission that we have been entrusted with.

Azurite

Formed by the oxidation of copper ores over time, Azurite is often found in combination with Malachite, which is also another copper-bearing stone. Azurite has become popular because of its unparalleled intense deep blue color. As a stone, it was considered sacred by both the ancient Egyptians as well as the Native Americans. In keeping, it has been used to create blue pigments for both paints and fabric dyes for eons.

Azurite is said to enhance inspiration and creativity, balancing both left and right sides of the brain to further awaken intuition and awareness.

At some point, all become the spiritual seeker.

If it is intensity of experience that you want, as in enhanced dreams and psychic abilities, then you have come to the right place, for we have been touted the stone of inner vision.

Healing the Planet and Ourselves

That having been said, you must be prepared for what you may experience, courtesy of our influence.

Do not be afraid, for we shall remain with you throughout the duration of your journey.

You may, however, wish to add another crystal companion or two, one for grounding and the other for protection. We shall not be the least bit insulted should you feel the need to do so.

We eagerly await your spiritual metamorphosis.

Mangano Calcite

Mangano Calcite derives its soft pink color from the direct presence of manganese within the stone. Calcite is a very common mineral, making up about 4% of the Earth's crust.

Pink Mangano Calcite is sometimes called the *Reiki Stone*. With a gentle but powerful energy, this stone has been touted as an excellent complement to energy healing modalities, such as Reiki, because of its excellent properties of energy amplification.

Pink is a color associated with the Heart chakra.

The Beatles have been touted as being one of the most successful and noteworthy bands of your age. Their songs about love, so catchy and upbeat, brought a smile to many faces, along with a lightness to many steps.

These are the very impressions that need to be recaptured in these trying times.

Healing the Planet and Ourselves

Created in love, you are the very essence of love. Fear, on the other hand, exists as the very opposite of love.

When you are engulfed in fear, you have lost the capacity to love in the truest (most pure) sense of the word.

Fear holds you captive to negative influences. Negative energies beget bondage. You are here to free yourself from this self-induced captivity.

As long as you continue to exist in fear, you are adding to the collective consciousness in a negative way.

You must take back your power; the power to think and act for yourself.

You have the power within yourself to relinquish the negative in order to wholeheartedly embrace the positive.

In a gentle, calming and soothing fashion, know that we are available to help facilitate what is needed.

Fulgurite

Fulgurites are actually natural hollow tubes of glass that are formed when lightning strikes sand (or any other such silica rich soil), causing the sand to melt. These pieces are formed in a single powerful event as compared to growing slowly over extended periods of time, as is the case with most crystals.

Given their creation, Fulgurites are said to resonate with a powerful source of heat and electricity. It is said, then, that these pieces can be used for both manifesting and focus.

You can expect to feel intense energies and have intense experiences when working steadily with us. We can be used, as glass would also be used, to magnify your clear intentions.

Feel free to avail of us when you want to manifest a particular vision you have for yourself, thereby allowing for an alchemical transformation, if you will.

Healing the Planet and Ourselves

It is said that we are a connection to the heavens from whence the lightening came that struck the sands of your world. Clearly, yin met yang with our creation.

As a specialty tool, we look forward to creating with you.

Garnet

Garnet is a gemstone that has been use since the Bronze Age, primarily as an abrasive at that time. There are actually six varieties of Garnet; hence, there are many colors of Garnet, including red, orange, yellow, green, blue, purple, brown, black, pink and colorless.

The red Garnets that I have worked with are called Almandine and Pyrope. With its deep, blood red color, Pyrope is the most famous form of Garnet. Almandine, on the other hand, is the most common, and most widely used, form of Garnet.

Red garnets were the most commonly used gemstones in the late Roman period, approximately 235-284 AD, close to the end of the 3rd century, just previous to what we refer to as the Middle Ages (from the 5th century to the 15th century).

Almandine was first documented by the Roman philosopher, Pliny the Elder, who named it after the ancient city of Alabanda in the Black Sea region of Turkey.

Through excavation, however, mankind has known of its existence since the Bronze Age. Almandine became very popular in the 18th century.

The German Emperor Otto had a carbuncle Almandine gemstone fitted to his crown. The Bohemian king, King Wenzel, had Pyrope gemstones fitted to his ceremonial attire.

Many of you feel no joy in this physical world. Taking a good hard look at the collective scenario, it is easy to see why this might be so.

We see our chief role as being one in which we can help our planetary brothers and sisters find joy amidst all of the chaos, all of the negativity, all of the confusion, that abounds in abundance.

As soon as you come to the realization that you have the power within you to control your thoughts, your words, your actions, you are on your way to experiencing this joy of which we speak.

Healing the Planet and Ourselves

Take the time to hold onto us as you work through the resolution to this overwhelming drama; for therein, so, too, will you reclaim your feelings of safety.

Much awaits you on the flip side of what appears to be the predominant state of affairs. Releasing yourself from this collective mindset is what necessitates its beginning.

Welcome to the world outside of the illusion.

Pyrite

Who has not heard of Fool's Gold?

Pyrite has been noted as being one of the stones used in history to produce fire. In the Middle Ages, alchemists thought they could turn Pyrite into Gold. Worn as a protective amulet for safety and good luck, it was also believed that Pyrite could heal ailments and injuries. Pyrite has been used in art and decoration for centuries.

It has been shared that Pyrite forms a protective shield around the wearer that deflects negativity. This gemstone is also said to align the meridians.

A most grounding stone, Pyrite can aid in the releasing of mental blocks. Likewise, it can assist in alleviating anxiety. Carrying a piece of Pyrite has long been recommended for individuals who are both studying and writing exams.

There are very few who have never been attracted to gold. The reasons, however, have been far from positive: power, control, greed.

Healing the Planet and Ourselves

We are a stone of warm, sunny and positive energies. You need not fight over us. You need not die to protect us.

We can instill you with the much needed confidence to take action on your ideas of inspiration.

In connecting you with the energy of the Earth, you will feel a sense of grounded contentment make its way through your physical body. Take the time to bask in these feelings of warmth and acceptance.

There is so much that you are here to accomplish.

Do not allow yourself to be controlled (disempowered) by another.

Unakite

Unakite was found in the Unaka Mountains situated in the southeastern United States. This most delightful looking gem consists of pink colored orthoclase Feldspar, Quartz and green Epidote. Some have also referred to this stone as Epidotized Granite. A relatively newly discovered stone, there is no extensive history to be found.

With the peachy pink and green colors (making it a most colorful stone related to the spring of the year), this is what makes it a good Heart chakra stone; a very calm, gentle, yet powerful (as well as uplifting and empowering) stone.

When one is balanced (united), the energies (feminine and masculine) work together.

It is essential that each of you find, and strive to maintain, this balance, for only then will you feel an acute sense of wholeness within your physical being.

Balance comes in many forms.

Healing the Planet and Ourselves

A balance of rest, diet and exercise, is what is needed for the physical body.

A balance of mindfulness, neutrality, living in the now and expressing love, is what is needed for the spiritual body.

A balance of alone time, engaging your passion and staying away from people that drain your energy, is what is needed for the emotional body.

A balance of letting go of the past, letting go of the need to be right, letting go of trying (because you have to just get out there and actually do it) and taking charge of your thinking and feelings through nonjudgmental observation (which is the same as mindfulness), is what is needed for the mental body.

When all systems are balanced, you can more successfully avoid the stressors that can run amuck, causing much grief and anguish on all four levels.

Now is the time to allow your balanced self to shine forth as a beacon of light to those who need your example from which to follow.

Healing the Planet and Ourselves

All will proceed accordingly.

You are to be commended on your unique accomplishments to date.

Green Tourmaline

Tourmaline comes in an amazing array of colors. Green Tourmaline stones can be found in a number of locations throughout the world including Afghanistan, Mozambique, Namibia, Nigeria and Pakistan, meaning that they are not a rare stone type. However, finding good quality pieces can be difficult.

Green Tourmaline is the second most expensive after Blue Indicolite. While the rarest color of Tourmaline is colorless, it is also the cheapest to buy.

We are a powerful healer for the physical heart, working to lessen the stress so often placed on this particular organ of the human body.

It is also imperative that you take other avenues to reduce stress, be they in the form of such mediums as ......

[1] engaging in yoga

[2] practicing meditation

Healing the Planet and Ourselves

[3] engaging in Tai Chi

[4] practicing Qigong

[5] listening to soothing music (especially the sounds of waterfalls)

[6] exercising on a daily basis

[7] using guided imagery

[8] focusing on aromatherapy

[9] utilizing breathing exercises

[10] focusing on progressive relaxation exercises

[11] taking a short walk

[12] taking a long vacation

[13] utilizing comedy (as in TV shows and movies) because laughter strengthens your immune system

[14] having a massage

[15] going for a reflexology session

[16] soaking in Epsom salts baths

[17] using light therapy

If you can lessen and/or eliminate unnecessary stress, you are on your way to strengthening the immune system response(s) of the body.

Surely a stronger, healthier body is the ultimate aim.

Pink Tourmaline

Tourmaline is one of the most fascinating of all gemstones, given its extensively wide range of colors. A bright and beautiful gem, Pink Tourmaline offers many choices when it comes to a specific shade of pink.

The first reference to the pyroelectric effect is made by Theophrastus in 314 BC, who noted that Tourmaline becomes charged when heated, thereby being able to attract straws and bits of wood. Theophrastus was the successor of Aristotle in the Peripatetic school (a school of philosophy) in ancient Greece.

The Empress Dowager, Tz'u Hsi of China, loved Pink Tourmaline and bought large quantities for gemstones and carvings from the then new Himalaya Mine, located in the Mesa Grande area of San Diego County, California (USA). Between 1902 and 1910, San Diego provided imperial China with 120 tons of gem-quality Pink Tourmaline.

Healing the Planet and Ourselves

Native Americans have used Pink and Green Tourmaline as funeral gifts for centuries.

We work to strengthen the link between the Heart chakra and the Crown chakra, thereby enabling the heart to become infused with expansive energies at the highest vibrational (some might even say divine) level.

With continued use, we are also able to provide a calming, centering type of fortitude, to the physical body.

Aligning your physical body with the energies of the Earth keeps one feeling grounded. When you are poorly grounded, your spatial understanding is impaired.

Imagine that you are a tree, extending your roots deep into the ground whereby you are better able to draw healing energies from the earth source itself.

Other grounding exercises include stomping your feet upon the ground, marching, walking barefoot while outside and doing squats.

Healing the Planet and Ourselves

To be grounded also means to be present in the here and now, connected clearly to your present identity, and in awareness of what is happening around you.

Remaining centered is key to achieving the all; by that we mean the body, mind and spirit balanced trine.

Watermelon Tourmaline

Watermelon Tourmaline, a naturally occurring gemsone, is a variety of Tourmaline that displays up to three different colors in the same crystal. In keeping with the fruit of the same name, they have green edges (the outer skin of the watermelon), a pink core (the sweet fruit) and white (the inner rind), which separates the two aforementioned colors. As you can tell, this particular variety of Tourmaline is most aptly named.

Aside from its most majestic look (as in the slice form), it is this particular crystal that can count itself amongst the most sought after crystals for working with the energies of the heart.

We are a synergistic and harmonious combination of both Green and Pink Tourmaline.

When you are innately attuned to joy, the natural condition of your BEing, you feel as if you are a composite whole.

Healing the Planet and Ourselves

In calming the mind, in calming the emotions, in soothing the heart, you find yourself open to this gift.

You are joy, you are love, you are compassion; this is what comprises the reality of who you really are.

It is in embracing, living from and adhering to, these very components that you are in a position to evolve on an exponential level.

Fossilized Dinosaur Bone

This particular fossil dates back to the Jurassic age, meaning 150+ million years ago. The piece that I work with was collected in North West Colorado (USA).

Metaphysically, Fossilized Dinosaur Bone is "known as the *Stone of Earth Changes and Evolution*. It helps us to realize that Change is a necessary event for Evolution to occur, and, that in one form or another, we will <u>all</u> survive intact. Energy cannot be destroyed, although it can change form endlessly. This is one of the lessons of Fossilized Dinosaur Bone." [37]

When I am feeling off center, without knowing why, I have a tendency to reach for this particular stone, knowing that I will soon begin to feel more centered, more grounded, more energized, more aligned.

---

[37] Words of Ravenia Youngman as per http://stores.ebay.ca/Crystal-Skull-Head-Quarters

Healing the Planet and Ourselves

An ancient stone, we represent life force energy. All of creation is imbued with the same life force energy; hence, everything, including us, including yourselves, is made of the same stuff (a fitting, but most inarticulate term, if we may say so).

If all is part of the same life force energy, an energy that gets recycled on a continuous basis, why, then, would you be afraid of the unknown? Can it not be said, therefore, that the unknown is merely a representation of who you are?

The chakras serve as gateways for the flow of this life force energy into your physical bodies. It is the openness of the chakras that determines the state of the flow of this energy, thereby determining your state of health and balance.

Mediums such as yoga and meditation serve to help balance out the energy of the chakras by purifying the lower energies and guiding them upwards. As the lower energies become harmonized with the higher energies at the level of the Heart chakra, you are then able to incorporate a heart-based approach to living.

Healing the Planet and Ourselves

Tai Chi integrates movement, breathing and meditation, a process that is intended to enhance the life force energy whilst uniting mind and body.

Orgone energy is the term used by psychoanalyst Wilhelm Reich to describe a universal life force, the primordial cosmic energy. This orgone is what the Chinese have long referred to as chi.

Reich proposed that orgone energy is everywhere and that it exists in two forms: positive orgone radiation (POR) and dead orgone radiation (DOR).

Positive orgone radiation is a life force energy that surrounds everything in its natural form.

By comparison, dead orgone radiation is produced by electromagnetic fields, microwaves, computers, cellular antennas and cell phones.

Dead orgone radiation is created when positive orgone radiation is killed off by electromagnetic pollution.

Healing the Planet and Ourselves

Electrical appliances emit deadly orgone, thereby exposing the human brain to disharmonious frequencies, causing electromagnetic stress. Constant exposure can cause lethargy, headaches and insomnia.

Reich determined that stacking alternating layers of fiberglass (which is an organic substance) and steel wool (which is an inorganic substance) would attract and collect both types of orgone energy.

Your Quantum physicists have proven the existence of orgone energy. So, too, have they proven that Reich's invention of orgone devices work on accumulating and transmuting unbalanced energy (DOR) into balanced energy (POR).

Made from cured fiberglass resin, metal chips, copper coils and crystals, Orgonite generators have the ability to capture orgone energy and reverse its negative polarity, healing all living things within its vicinity.

In summation, orgonite transforms dead orgone into positive orgone.

Healing the Planet and Ourselves

Such is a most inexpensive way to help restore balance to the Earth. In keeping, orgonite can strengthen the aura and protect one against negativity, stress and electromagnetic field radiation.

Orgonite is commonly being used by practitioners of Geomancy and Feng Shui for correcting energy imbalances. In short, this simple and subtle technology is improving the energetic quality of your environment.

Azeztulite

The stone Azeztulite continues to be one located at the center of gemstone controversy.

According to Robert Simmons, "Azeztulite is quartz. From the strictly materialistic point of view, that is the end of it, and in my writings over the past fifteen years, I have been saying that Azeztulite is quartz. However, for those interested in the metaphysical side of things, there is much more to the story. Energetically, although Azeztulite is quartz, not all quartz is Azeztulite." [38]

As is also shared, "if people say Azeztulite is chemically something other than quartz, that is untrue. However, when they say that certain quartz stones have different energetic qualities than others, and that certain subjectively felt currents identify a stone as Azeztulite, that is something

---

[38] Simmons, Robert. *Is Azeztulite For Real?* article accessed on January 20, 2011 and located on the Heaven and Earth LLC website at http://heavenandearthjewelry.com/

Healing the Planet and Ourselves

which can only be determined by experience, since we have no machines capable of measuring the spiritual energies of stones." [39]

Spiritual evolution is the reason why you have come, why you are here now.

To evolve into the highest form has long been your undertaking, for this shall mean that you will have finally attained complete and total freedom from that which attempts to confine and restrict you from exhibiting your truest nature.

Nonjudgment is the way to remembering the sacredness of all life.

As you become aware of your limiting beliefs, you better understand that your interactions with others are driven by what you believe to be true about the person.

---

[39] Simmons, Robert. *Is Azeztulite For Real?* article accessed on January 20, 2011 and located on the Heaven and Earth LLC website at http://heavenandearthjewelry.com/

Healing the Planet and Ourselves

Sadly, these limiting beliefs never reflect the actual truth, a truth that states all is one.

As you gain in universal awareness, you quickly come to the realization that your divinity is also theirs as well. When you remember, embrace and share your divinity, you free others to walk their truth. You become accepting of their truth, for such is whom they are.

It is our privilege to work with you in this capacity.

With wings, all can fly, can they not?

Citrine Azeztulite

Citrine Azeztulite, which comes in the form of a crystal point, is a recent find from North Caroline (USA). It is also known by its trademark name, Golden Azeztulite.

It is said that these Golden Azeztulite crystals emanate the pure golden light of the great central Sun, thereby supporting our evolutionary transformation into Human Beings of Light. [40]

We are here to tell you that all is not lost, as difficult as this may be for some to accept. You are incredibly powerful beings, more powerful, in fact, than you have ever dreamed, but most of you are still asleep to that which constitutes the real you.

We are here to support you in waking up from the illusion to the reality.

---

[40] Information obtained through the Heaven and Earth LLC website accessed on January 20, 2011 at http://heavenandearthjewelry.com/

Healing the Planet and Ourselves

In becoming aware that one is asleep, they are already enroute to their glorious awakening.

The first thing that needs to happen is the recognition that you are the controller (operator) of your thoughts, words and actions; that no one makes you respond in any given way to anything. Instead, your response always results from a choice that you have made.

It becomes in reaching this sublevel of understanding that you will already have achieved something of monumental importance.

You can only work up from there because you will also have realized the significance of reclaiming your personal power, thereby taking back total responsibility for your life.

As Messengers of Light, we are here to help facilitate your evolution as spiritual human beings at this most exciting time.

We look forward to working with you on this endeavor of great import.

Left and Right Activation Crystal

Left Activation crystals are recognized by an inclined window located on the *left* side of the primary face of the crystal. They primarily activate and increase performance of left brain function. It is also believed that they can be used to access information from the past.

Right Activation crystals are recognized by an inclined window located on the *right* side of the primary face of the crystal. They primarily activate and increase performance of right brain function. It is also believed that they can be used to access information from the future.

Left and Right Activation crystals encourage a melding of both right and left brain abilities, bringing about a synthesis of same. It is far easier to purchase each activation type crystal, singularly, using both to work together.

While I cannot speak as to the rarity of such a find, I was, however, most fortunate to acquire a single crystal piece that features both inclined window formations.

Healing the Planet and Ourselves

Lateralization of the brain continues to be evident in the phenomena that can be demonstrated between right handedness and left handedness, as well as brain dominance.

The left hemisphere specializes in analytical thought (logic, discipline, rules, deductive reasoning, knowledge, details, strategy, planning, goals, practicality and safety).

The right hemisphere specializes in intuitive based thought (feelings, emotions, daydreaming, big picture oriented, visualization, creativity, spatial awareness, spontaneity, risk taking, flexibility, philosophical thought and learning through experience).

The balancing of both hemispheres of the brain serves to optimize one's physical health, while also enhancing the performance of both mind and body.

While your mental state affects your brainwaves, the opposite is also true, meaning that your brainwaves affect your mental state.

Healing the Planet and Ourselves

What this essentially means is that you can actually control your mental state by controlling your brainwaves.

This is the technology that exists behind Brainwave Entrainment.

We suggest that you work with us for small time periods in the beginning, increasing your involvement in small increments, as it is possible that you may develop headaches from working with us (a clear sign that we are doing what we are supposed to be doing).

Lithium Based Stones

There are many medications being used to treat a range of anxiety disorders, including bipolar disorder. These medications have been found to contain lithium. Research seems to indicate that lithium can also help to reduce the effects of Alzheimer's disease.

There are many stones that contain lithium, such as ……

Lithium Quartz (varying percentages)

Petalite (2 to 4 percent)

Lepidolite (3 to 5 percent)

Spodumene (4 to 8 percent)

Kunzite (8 to 8.5 percent) also known as Pink Spodumene

Hiddenite (8 to 8.5 percent) also known as Green Spodume

Amblygonite (8 to 10 percent)

Golden C (up to 35 percent)

Healing the Planet and Ourselves

In keeping with current scientific understanding, perhaps there might well be some added benefit to carrying some of these stones upon the physical body. In accordance with research from <u>Lithium and Lithium Stones</u> by Haroldine as well as the <u>ABC's of Crystals</u> by Elaine Finster, there are a number of uses attributed to lithium [41] that the reader can seek out for themselves.

Disclaimer

The information contained herein is neither a prescription nor a diagnostic alternative. It is quite possible that while crystals do not heal, they may aid the physical body in the healing of itself. In accessing metaphysical information, the reader both acknowledges and agrees that he/she personally assumes all responsibility for their use of this information.

---

[41] *Lithium Research* article retrieved on August 3, 2010 at http://www.luminanti.com/goldenc.html#anchor443561

Nano Wand

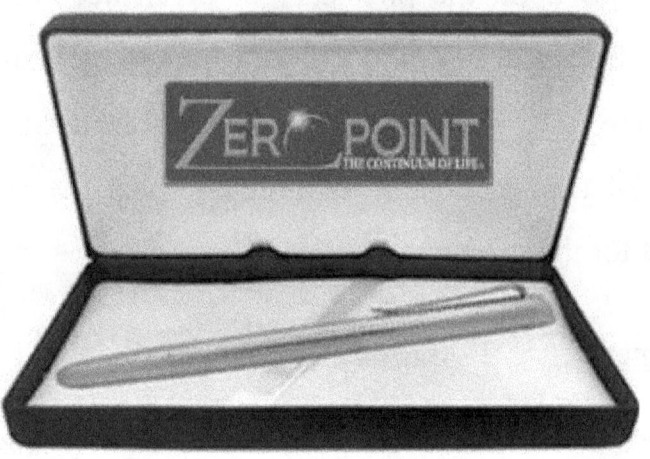

All matter is comprised of energy. Zero Point energy is formless. Zero Point energy is also the source of everything. Tachyon Energy was the first to emerge out of the energetic continuum. Tachyon energy cannot be measured. It is not limited to a certain frequency.

Everything that transpires within the human body is already encoded within Tachyon energy (or chi) in perfect form, meaning that Tachyon represents a safe and most natural possibility for enabling the human body to move back to energetic health and balance.

Healing the Planet and Ourselves

I am currently involved in exploring Zero Point energy via the Zero Point Continuum of Life Nano Wand. [42]

The result of more than 27 years of research, and based on a synergy of ancient healing wisdom and modern scientific breakthroughs, these powerful Nano Wands are comprised of a proprietary scientific combination of granulated minerals, fused together inside a magnetic casing (of high grade stainless steel) to access Zero Point energy.

The Nano Wand contains Zeolite, Tourmaline, Germanium, Magnetite, Hematite, Rose Quartz, Amethyst and a proprietary blend of more than forty other crystals, minerals and elemental ingredients, all of which support the process of scalar energy healing.

The Nano Wand is a natural energy generating device that rejuvenates molecular structures found in all liquids.

---

[42] http://zeropointbreakthrough.com/reps/mdoucette/

Healing the Planet and Ourselves

With the human body ranging anywhere from 55% to 78% water, depending on physical size, water is the medium that enables the signal of the beneficial energy patterns from the Nano Wand to improve the quality of the body's liquids.

The Nano Wand facilitates and strengthens the flow of bio-energy (also called chi or ki). It also unblocks areas in which that energy may not be flowing fully. This can have the effect of allowing your body to improve its natural immune response, thereby increasing energy. In addition, the nutrients and micronutrients in the foods you consume can be more effectively utilized.

The Zero Point Continuum of Life Nano Wand is fully endorsed by the Centre for Quantum Healing & Noetic Sciences in Lancaster, Pennsylvania (USA).

The Continuum of Sound®

Let's get this right, straight away. There is no them, there is no us. While the universe appears to be dualistic in nature, merely to help you better understand that which you want versus that which you do not want, which is part of the illusion that you agreed to, eventually all come to understand that nonduality is key. There is only Source; hence, there is only we.

Everything is comprised of energy. Everything is vibration. All vibration is the result of energy in motion. Energy is held together to create matter. Matter is energy condensed to a slow vibration.

Of course, this means that everything in the universe (every object, every being, every thought, every action, every psychological mood) has a unique vibrational energy.

In short, energy equals vibration.

Healing the Planet and Ourselves

Taking it one step further, so, too, is sound vibration. Mind (consciousness) influences energy, which is, of course, vibration.

Vibration, in the form of sound, is known to have a profound effect on one's consciousness.

This can only be achieved, however, when sound has reached a certain frequency level. Mind you, it also has to be presented in the proper format.

When you think about mantras, chanting, the beating of drums; all of these can be used to alter states of consciousness via sound, can they not?

Brainwave Entrainment appears to be their modern day correspondent.

Clearly, then, the vibration of sound can serve to raise your vibrational level; the higher your vibration, the easier it becomes to manifest, thereby achieving all that can possibly be desired.

Healing the Planet and Ourselves

While visualization, affirmation and meditation serve to assist some in their journey, in truth, it is the vibration of sound that demonstrates the most intensity towards this realization, for this further serves to assist one in actualizing the God within; this is when enlightenment has been attained.

It is my personal belief, as well as experience, that a series of acoustic frequencies, developed to inspire healing, can serve to create an extremely powerful meditative environment whereby the mind (consciousness) can be affected in a most profound way.

Truth be told, the science of vibrational healing is not new. For thousands of years, in nearly every culture, there have been hands-on-healers who have utilized the healing frequencies found in nature.

It has been said that Beta waves can be likened to the frequency of the conscious mind. By comparison, then, both Alpha and Theta waves constitute the subconscious mind.

Healing the Planet and Ourselves

This, then, means that the more one is able to relax, the slower their brainwaves become (of course, you say) and the *more open you become* to Source.

Having experimented with much in the form of Brainwave Entrainment, I am now finding the Continuum of Sound® acoustic frequencies [43] to be the answer for myself.

---

[43] http://zeropointbreakthrough.com/reps/mdoucette/

Astrology Related

No doubt many of you will have heard about specific planets being in retrograde. What exactly does this mean?

Mira Bai, a friend of mine, shares a rather succinct explanation. [44]

There are three definitions of a planet's rotation and/or movement; namely, retrograde, station, and direct.

A retrograde is when a planet appears to be moving or rotating backwards. This, she tells me, is really an optical illusion of sorts created by the orbital rotation of Earth in relation to the location of the other planets, with the best example being to compare a retrograde to driving down the highway. A car is beside you in the next lane. All of a sudden, it slows down while you continue the same speed and motion. This is the optical illusion.

---

[44] Huggins, Kristi. *Mercury in Retrograde: Crystals That Can Help* article retrieved on August 1, 2010 and located at http://www.healingcrystals.com/Mercury_in_Retrograde-_Crystals_that_can_help_Articles_1686.html

Healing the Planet and Ourselves

So, for a Mercury in Retrograde, for example, the Earth is simply speeding by, passing the planet, which, in turn, makes it appear to be going backwards.

Station refers to when the planet appears to slow to a stop, with no visible movement (another optical illusion).

Direct, or "going Direct" means that the planet appears to change direction, rotating properly once again.

She also cites numerous crystals that can be of assistance during such astrologically related times.

To achieve increased focus and concentration levels: Citrine, Moss Agate, Smoky Quartz or Citrine.

For feelings of additional peace, security and patience: Blue Lace Agate, Celestite, Turquoise, Chrysocolla, Petalite or Sugilite.

To achieve relaxation: Amethyst, Blue Calcite, Charoite, Dumortierite, Obsidian, Selenite, Emerald or Rose Quartz.

When wanting to bring in the energy of your new and improved positive intent: Cavansite, Larimar or Blue Topaz.

Healing the Planet and Ourselves

To stabilize and balance electronic devices during a retrograde time: Moss Agate or Obsidian.

To keep you and your electronic devices grounded: Red Jasper, Hematite or Black Tourmaline.

To keep lines of communication open and cleared: Blue Kyanite, Blue Calcite, Labradorite or Lapis Lazuli.

To remove the energy of chaos that surrounds you: Pyrite.

To ease one's anxiety, thereby providing a greater sense of organization: Howlite, Lepidolite, Moonstone or Rutilated Quartz.

To keep your focus from wandering in a different direction: Ametrine, Fluorite or Ruby.

To experience re-centeredness when nothing is working out as it should: Selenite.

Healing the Planet and Ourselves

To learn more about Mira Bai, author, teacher and personal crystal consultant, please take the time to visit her website: MoonCave Crystals Creative Designs©. [45]

---

[45] http://www.mooncavecrystals.com/

Metaphysical Property Sites

This particular text does not delve into the metaphysical properties attributed to crystals and stones. Some of the sites that I frequent, in reference to this knowledge, are:

Metaphysical Properties: Heaven and Earth [46]

Metaphysical, New Age and Crystal Healing Information [47]

Therapeutic Gemstones for Healing and Awakening [48]

Gemstone Healing Properties at Charms of Light [49]

Spirit of Isis Crystal Database [50]

---

[46] http://www.heavenandearthjewelry.com/Raw-Tumbles-Stones.aspx
[47] http://www.crystalsandjewelry.com/metaphysicalproperties.html
[48] http://www.gemisphere.com/gemstones/therapeutic_gemstones.htm
[49] http://www.charmsoflight.com/healing/gemstone-properties.html
[50] http://www.spiritofisis.org/index_files/info_crystals.htm

Crystals and Crystal Healing Information [51]

Crystal Vaults: Quartz Crystals, Their Identification and Meanings [52]

Good Vibrations Crystals [53]

The Quartz Page: Growth Forms [54]

That Crystal Site [55]

Peaceful Mind: Crystal and Gemstone Therapy [56]

Disclaimer

Metaphysical and healing lore in reference to crystal meanings is for inspiration, folklore, reference and entertainment purposes only.

---

[51] http://www.crystalreflection.co.uk/information-crystals-and-healing.asp
[52] http://www.crystalvaults.com/pages/quartz_crystals_explained.php
[53] http://www.goodvibrationscrystals.com/guide_to_crystals.asp
[54] http://www.quartzpage.de/gro_text.html
[55] http://www.thatcrystalsite.com/guide/properties-glossary.php
[56] http://www.peacefulmind.com/stones.htm

Concluding Message

For some reason, I am attracted to many ancient stones, most notably [1] Nuummite (about 3 billion years old), [2] Anorthosite (perhaps as old as Nuummite), [3] Herkimer Diamonds (perhaps about 400 to 500 million years old), [4] Libyan Desert Glass, also known as LDG (about 30 million years old) and [5] Moldavite (about 15 million years old).

What this means, I cannot say. It could mean that I am an old soul that has lived countless lives on the face of this planet. In truth, one must always pay attention to that which one resonates with.

Hopefully you have been able to discern, courtesy of these special messages, that we have co-created everything that exists.

Together we share (and have always shared) a common denominator ... the divine part of us (spirit) that dwells within all that is.

Our collective challenge "is to share knowledge, allowing us to save the planet from ourselves. We are at war from within and without you see, because we do not recall who ... we truly are." [57]

Having become entrapped by materialism (in direct connection with the five senses), we have become mere shadows of our former selves as powerful creators, as powerful spiritual beings.

Here is something else to ponder.

The laws of physics dictate "that every action has an equal and opposing reaction. A philosophical version of this law would be that if humans are capable of killing the planet, it must be because they once played an active part in bringing it to life." [58]

By now, many of you will have become aware that everything in the cosmos is connected. Unfortunately, most individuals may not yet be privy to this cultural mindset.

---

[57] Wuttunnee, Stéphane. *Dreaming the Pyramid* ebook (page 18).
[58] Ibid.

Healing the Planet and Ourselves

It is atrocities such as "wars, environmental degradation, murders, suicides, and social intolerance [that] should be fiction to the world, not fact." [59]

In order to become more spiritually aware, in order to realize just how connected you are with every individual soul, you must first look to yourself because change can only start from within.

An immense task, it must be wholeheartedly embraced.

Every human being "is an adventurer – a courageous soul who willingly chooses to come to Earth to fulfill some type of important mission for humanity." [60] Nothing can be more important than understanding who we *truly* are.

Awareness and respect are key factors. As we change in our continued and ever growing spiritual and intuitive understandings, so, too, will Mother Gaia respond accordingly; in essence, it really does come down to us.

---

[59] Wuttunnee, Stéphane. *Dreaming the Pyramid* ebook (pages 22-23).
[60] Ibid, page 116.

Healing the Planet and Ourselves

In remembering that we are co-creators, whatever is conceivable in the mind inevitably manifests in the physical world. We are here to manifest the reality of creating a heaven on earth.

On an individual journey, each is here to heal their wounded selves. Through compassionate allowing and nonjudgment, you become "a Messiah unto Yourself." [61] Having done so, each can successfully lead by their own example.

Crystals can be found everywhere in the world – in the snow (snowflakes), in the ice (crystallized water), in the ground. Could it not be said, then, that the Earth, herself, is like a giant crystal?

Given the water and liquid blood (infused with necessary minerals and elements) contained within the human body, we, too, are crystallized beings.

In the most basic of terms, crystals are both receivers and transmitters of energy.

---

[61] Wuttunnee, Stéphane. *Dreaming the Pyramid* ebook (page 139).

Healing the Planet and Ourselves

The energy a crystal receives "can be sound and radio frequencies, brainwaves, emotions, sights, smells, and so on. Depending on how we reconfigure our inner crystals through prayer, meditation, and intention, the end result of how the energy emits from us will vary." [62]

As human crystal receivers and transmitters, it is important to control the type types of energy that we expose ourselves to. We can heal ourselves with the power of love and positive thinking, if that is our choice. So, too, can we continue to exist in the depths of despair, via negative thoughts.

We become that which we focus on. As a man thinketh, so shall he be. So, how can we program ourselves to think in a more positive and accepting manner?

The easiest way to do this is "by flooding the mind, positive brainwashing if you will, with powerful imagery, scents and sounds – whatever it takes to make us think deeply about life and love. You want to change your life? Change your

---

[62] Wuttunnee, Stéphane. *Dreaming the Pyramid* ebook (page 187).

thinking by flooding yourself with positive influences and thoughts. Stop hanging around negative people if all they want to do is leech off of you and your energy. Do not watch the news if it makes you sad. Spend some meditative time everyday speaking and listening to your best friend; yourself. Post little happy notes and images all over the house until you actually become that reality." [63]

The energies surrounding the planet are continuing to accelerate and all are affected. Many are feeling the effects of this change in ways that most would consider negative: life-threatening illnesses, incurable diseases, heated tempers, out of character behavior, unreasonable actions, irritabilty, depression and despair.

If you find yourself identifying with these words, take heart. What most may not understand is that unless such negativities are purged and released, we cannot hope to create the balanced state that is needed. Detached strength, tolerance and understanding are key.

---

[63] Wuttunnee, Stéphane. *Dreaming the Pyramid* ebook (page 192).

Healing the Planet and Ourselves

Do not be "inclined to feelings of despair in the wake of such inevitable crises [political upheaval, wars, uprisings, mass turmoil and chaos]. For the end result, the establishment of positivity on the planet, would have been achieved in the process. Tune into the feelings that arise within you during these times, and strive to maintain harmony within your home, your workplace, and within your heart. For this level of balance is a key factor in doing your part to modify the negative effects in your own immediate surroundings." [64]

Much can be accomplished "on an individual basis in the coming times. Strive to keep focused on maintaining harmony within and in your interactions with others. Avoid confrontations and expressions of inner discord. Practice discernment in your assessment of the behavior of others prior to reacting to behavior that may not be based on circumstance, but on energy assimilation. Learn to distinguish between what is logically the result of considered, thought-directed action and what is not.

---

[64] Rasha. (1998) The Calling (page 92). Santa Fe, NM: Earthstar Press.

Healing the Planet and Ourselves

Moreover, act with compassion and with love toward all your fellow beings and creatures. For in so doing, you will make the greatest possible contribution in the coming times." [65]

Eros, or the creative dimension of God, is that burning intelligence and driving impulse that is ever-leaning forward, reaching toward the emergence of that which has not yet become manifest. Evolutionary Enlightenment is about unapologetically becoming a living embodiment of those values that create the conditions for that unselfconscious creativity at the very edge of the possible. Andrew Cohen, editor of EnlightenNext Magazine

Thank you for sharing your precious time with me. I trust that there have been messages herein that have resonated within your soul. In paying attention to these feelings, you will have rediscovered your inner truth.

Namaste.

---

[65] Rasha. (1998) The Calling (page 92). Santa Fe, NM: Earthstar Press.

Bibliography

Ambose, Kala. (2007) *9 Life Altering Lessons: Secrets of the Mystery Schools Unveiled.*

Bunick, Nick. (2010) *Time for Truth: A New Beginning.*

Chopra, Deepak. (2005) *Peace Is The Way: Bringing War and Violence to An End.*

Coelho, Paulo. (1998) *The Alchemist.*

Coelho, Paulo. (2003) *Warrior of The Light.*

Doucette, Michele. (2010) *A Travel in Time to Grand Pré* (second edition).

Doucette, Michele. (2010) *The Ultimate Enlightenment For 2012: All We Need Is Ourselves.*

Doucette, Michele. (2010) *Turn Off The TV: Turn On Your Mind.*

Doucette, Michele. (2010) *Veracity At Its Best.*

Doucette, Michele. (2010) *Sleepers Awaken. The Time Is Now To Consciously Create Your Own Reality.*

Gawain, Shakti. (1998) *Living In The Light: A Guide to Personal and Planetary Transformation* (second edition).

Hansard, Christopher. (2003) *The Tibetan Art of Positive Thinking.*

Harris, Philip F. *Jesus Taught It Too: The Early Roots of the Law of Attraction* located online at http://www.psitek.net/pages/PsiTek-jesus-taught-it-too-1.html

Kribbe, Pamela. (2008) *The Jeshua Channelings: Christ Consciousness in a New Era.*

Kybalion (a study of Hermetic philosophy pertaining to both ancient Egypt and ancient Greece)

McTaggart, Lynne. (2003) *The Field: The Quest For The Secret Force Of The Universe.*

McTaggart, Lynne. (2008) *The Intention Experiment: Using Your Thoughts to Change Your Life and the World.*

Rasha. (1998) *The Calling*.

Rasha. (2006) *Oneness*.

Tolle, Eckhart. (2005) *A New Earth: Awakening to Your Life's Purpose*.

White, Mary Mageau. *Preparing for Ascension* e-book (an interactive study course).

White, Mary Mageau. *Our Chakra System: A Portal to Interdimensional Consciousness* e-book.

Wuttunnee, Stéphane. *Dreaming the Pyramid* e-book.

NOTE

The resources listed herein as written by both Mary Mageau White and Stéphane Wuttunnee can be gleaned, free of charge, from the author herself.

Healing the Planet and Ourselves

2010 in Review (Live Kryon Channeling)
http://www.kryon.com/k_channel10_dallas.html

Dr. Suzan Carroll (free inspirational books)
http://www.multidimensions.com/TheVision/books.html

Articles on Personal and Planetary Transformation
http://www.kachina.net/~alunajoy/articles.html

A Society of Souls ~ The School for Nondual Healing and Awakening
http://www.kabbalah.org/

Awakening Earth (Duane Elgin)
http://www.awakeningearth.org/

Becoming ONE, People and Planet: A Manual for Personal and Planetary Transformation Volumes 1 and 2
http://www.becomingone-book.com/freedownload.htm

Becoming The Human Crystal: Manifesting Personal and Planetary Transformation
http://becomingthehumancrystal.com/

California Institute of Integral Studies: Philosophy, Cosmology and Consciousness Programs
http://www.ciis.edu/Academics/Graduate_Programs/Philosophy_Cosmology_and_Consciousness_.html

Dharma Rain Zen Center
http://www.dharma-rain.org/?p=practice_zazen

EnlightenNext: The Teachings of Andrew Cohen
http://www.enlightennext.org/andrew/

EnlightenNext Magazine: The Magazine for Revolutionaries
http://www.enlightennext.org/magazine/

Foundation for Conscious Evolution
http://www.barbaramarxhubbard.com/con/

Gaia Mind
http://www.gaiamind.org/

Galactic Time Cycles for Personal and Planetary Transformation
http://www.13moon.com/

Healing the Planet and Ourselves

Institute of Noetic Sciences
http://noetic.org/

Integral Institute (Ken Wilber)
http://in.integralinstitute.org/

Integral Review: A Transdisciplinary and Transcultural Journal For New Thought, Research and Praxis
http://integral-review.org/

Kheper: transformation, evolution, metamorphosis
http://www.kheper.net/index.htm

Love is the New Religion (The Spiritual Conspiracy)
http://brianpiergrossi.com/blog/shareit/

Multidimenional Meditations (Dr. Suzan Carroll)
http://www.multidimensions.com/TheVision/meditationdownloads.html

Mystic Mindpower (Jody Sachse)
It is here that you will find several Zen based meditations worth purchasing.
http://www.mysticmindpower.com/products.html

Nonduality (Jerry Katz)
http://www.nonduality.com/

Ode Magazine: The Online Community for Intelligent Optimists
http://www.odemagazine.com/

Personal and Planetary Transformation with Sound and Sacred Geometry
http://www.dreamweaving.com/

Principles of Sacred Consciousness
http://sacredworld.net/Principles/prin-purpose.htm

Purification Image (Véronique Blommaart)
http://www.share-purification.com/purification/eng.htm

Spirit of Now (Peter Russell)
http://www.peterrussell.com/index2.php

Spiritual Endeavors: Many Paths, One Destination
http://www.spiritual-endeavors.org/

Ten Steps to Personal Transformation
http://www.byregion.net/articles-healers/tensteps.html

Healing the Planet and Ourselves

The Club of Budapest
http://www.clubofbudapest.org/index.php

The Graduate Institute: Conscious Evolution
http://www.learn.edu/ce

The Journal of Conscious Evolution
http://www.cejournal.org/index.html

The Planetary Transformation Project
http://www.facebook.com/pages/The-Planetary-Transformation-Project/113350028721169

The Sounds of Our Planet series (King Tet® Productions)
Eric Van der Wyk
http://soundsofourplanet.com/

The Wisdom Blog (Christian de Quincey)
http://thewisdomblog.wordpress.com/

Tom Fitzgerald: Being Present Awareness
http://www.tomfitzgerald.org/philosophy/index.html

Healing the Planet and Ourselves

Whole Person, Whole Planet: Personal Transformation Creates Planetary Transformation
http://www.wholepersonwholeplanet.com/

World Blessings: Holding the Light for a Sacred Earth
http://www.worldblessings.com/

About the Author

Michele Doucette is webmistress of Portals of Spirit, a spirituality website whereby one will find links to (1) The Enlightened Scribe, (2) an ezine called Gateway To The Soul, (3) books of spiritual resonance as well as authors of metaphysical importance, (4) categories of interest from Angels to Zen, (5) up-to-date information as shared by a Quantum Healer, (6) affiliate programs and resources of personal significance, (7) healing resource advertisements and (8) spiritual news.

As a Level 2 Reiki Practitioner, she sends long distance Reiki to those who make the request, claiming only to be a facilitator of the Universal energy, meaning that it is up to the individual(s) in question to use these energies in order to heal themselves.

Having also acquired a Crystal Healing Practitioner diploma (Stonebridge College in the UK), she is guardian to many from the mineral kingdom.

She is the author of several spiritual/metaphysical works; namely, *The Ultimate Enlightenment For 2012: All We Need Is Ourselves*, *Turn Off The TV: Turn On Your Mind*, *Veracity At Its Best*, *The Collective: Essays on Reality* (a composition of essays in relation to the Matrix) and *Sleepers Awaken: The Time Is Now To Consciously Create Your Own Reality*, all of which have been published through St. Clair Publications. In addition, she has written a volume that deals with crystals, aptly entitled *The Wisdom of Crystals*.

She is also the author of *A Travel in Time to Grand Pré*, a visionary metaphysical novel that historically ties the descendants of Yeshua (Jesus) to modern day Nova Scotia. As shared by a reviewer, *Veracity At Its Best* "constructs the context for the spiritual message" imparted in *A Travel in Time to Grand Pré*.

Against the backdrop of 1754 Acadie, it was the blending of French Acadian history with current DNA testing that contributed to the weaving of this alchemical tale of time travel, romance and intrigue.

Healing the Planet and Ourselves

From Henry I Sinclair to the Merovinglans, from the Cathari treasure at Montségur to the Knights Templar, this novel, together with the words of Yeshua as spoken at the height of his ministry, has the potential to inspire others; for it is herein that we learn how individuals can find their way, their truth(s), so as to live their lives to the fullest.

www.ingramcontent.com/pod-product-compliance
Lightning Source LLC
Chambersburg PA
CBHW060450090426
42735CB00011B/1959